BIG-GAME TAXIDERMY

Books by Todd Triplett

The Complete Book of Wild Hog Hunting
The Complete Guide to Waterfowl Taxidermy
The Complete Guide to Upland Game Bird Taxidermy
The Complete Guide to Small Game Taxidermy

BIG-GAME TAXIDERMY
A Complete Guide to Deer, Antelope, and Elk

Todd Triplett

The Lyons Press
Guilford, Connecticut
An imprint of The Globe Pequot Press

This book is dedicated to my dad, Harry Triplett, who provided my first opportunity to view the process of big-game taxidermy in a most refined form.

The Lyons Press is an imprint of The Globe Pequot Press.

10 9 8 7 6 5 4 3 2 1

Printed in the United States of America

ISBN-13: 978-1-59228-880-9
ISBN-10: 1-59228-880-4

Library of Congress Cataloging-in-Publication Data is available on file.

Contents

Preface: An Elk Hunt

As we sat together taking in the beautiful scenery, my guide, Gabriel Jackson, and I seized the opportunity for a water break. After a few minutes of rest, Gabriel pulled a GPS unit from his pack. Once he had acquired our position, he said that we had climbed 1,600 vertical feet from our starting point, over a mile and a half away. The terrain that we had covered was rough stuff, with loose shale and lava rock scattered about the surface of the ground. This was certainly not what one expects when hunting elk, but Gabriel assured me that the area was home to not only an abundance of elk, but also to some true giants as well.

It was very easy to understand why Gabriel was so confident about this area, as he told tales of bulls scoring well over the four-hundred mark taken each year from the San Carlos Apache Reservation. During the previous year Gabriel had personally taken a nice bull in the Malay Gap area in a late-season rifle hunt. The elk narrowly missed the 370-inch mark. With all of the trophy bulls around, the Malay Gap was possibly the most reasonably priced elk tag in the country, where a hunter might find himself with a chance at a 350-class bull. Truth be told, I was sitting smack-dab in the middle of possibly the best trophy elk country in the world. Another advantage I had was the fact that I was accompanied by one of the best elk guides available on the San Carlos. Gabriel seemed to have a love for elk hunting that was rivaled only by his love for his family.

After catching our breath, we began glassing the canyon bottom. According to Gabriel, the bulls had formed small bachelor groups, and during this late season, would feed throughout the night. Then, they would make their way into the cool cover of the pinyon-juniper trees scattered along the creek drainages where they would spend most of the day before starting their next nighttime feed.

Gabriel soon dropped his binoculars and motioned toward the bottom of the canyon. Two separate groups of two bulls each were slowly making their way to a resting spot. One elk that stopped to nibble on a prickly pear cactus appeared to be almost 325 inches, and though he wasn't a top-end Malay Gap bull, he was a mature animal. This was the last day of our hunt and I decided this bull was the one. We quickly hatched a plan and began our descent into the drainage where the bulls would be resting.

Our approach down the steep hillside took over an hour, coursing over the same scattered rock that lay everywhere else we had ventured. At last we were at the backbone of the ridge that hid the bull's resting spot. After a short discussion, I decided to sit tight while Gabriel dropped lower on the ridgetop in hopes of spotting the bedded bulls, at which time he would return and we would approach the bulls together. But things didn't work out quite as planned.

Moments after leaving my sight, I heard Gabriel making several loud cow calls. Knowing that my guide would cow-call quietly if he had slipped on some rocks or made some other noise, the louder, more numerous cow calls meant something extraordinary was afoot. My ears perked up and my adrenaline started to flow when I heard rock and shale rolling along the hillside as if something was making a hasty getaway. I turned and spotted two large racks sticking out from the juniper and other foliage, and watched as two bulls made their escape from the creek drainage. Moments later, the nice bull that we had spotted from the canyon rim was standing, angling away from my location.

I quickly used my shooting sticks to center the crosshairs of my T/C Encore .300 Magnum on the near shoulder of the elk. I steadied myself and squeezed the trigger. The rifle cracked and almost simultaneously, the large animal collapsed.

After a brief session of high fives and back slapping, we slowly made our way to my trophy that lay amidst the thick undergrowth. He was a seven-point bull that grossed just over 320 inches. I was ecstatic.

Momentarily, my mind reeled back to my first big-game animal, a spike whitetail buck taken at the age of fourteen in

North Carolina while hunting with my late grandfather. I felt as proud looking over my elk now as I had then, when I was just a kid with his first buck.

These few moments of recollection were followed by the taking of several photographs and the regimen of skinning and butchering. We strapped on our packs, now filled with meat, and headed toward the truck. Even after three miles and a 1,600-foot climb and descent, we were still smiling as we loaded my prize onto the truck.

For more information on hunting the San Carlos Apache Tribe, see Appendix B.

This hunt was simply one of many that I have been fortunate enough to experience while traipsing through forests and fields. It was definitely a hunt that I will remember and cherish, second only to taking that first deer. The serious sportsman or big-game hunter knows well the meaning and gratification of such an endeavor, and certainly understands my feelings about what I do. My desire to preserve as trophies the best animals I take comes from my deep-seated love of the hunt.

Big-game taxidermy has a long history, with some evidence suggesting that the art of preserving trophy animals has been around for several hundred years. A century ago, the most common method for commercial mounting went as follows: Once the skin was preserved, it was then pulled upon a structure built from wood surrounded by excelsior—wood wool, clay, or most any medium on hand that would create a near-natural shape of the animal. Typically, the actual skull of the animal was used, and clay was employed to create the musculature around the skull. Early methods were crude to say the least, but there were those pioneers who carefully studied and measured each section of a carcass until they had a very full understanding of skeletal structures and musculature, at which point they created very realistic, lifelike molds from clay. The clay was then allowed to dry and the mounting procedure was completed. Those who ventured into this type of taxidermy were eons ahead of the competition, but a quest for fame and fortune wasn't the reason they worked so hard at trying to achieve perfection. These taxidermy geniuses were simply attempting to expand the horizons of this relatively primitive skill, while providing museums and other big-game hunters with the most realistic result possible. Big-game taxidermy has always been and will continue to be an art that embellishes and extends our time in the field, celebrating the beauty and life of the animals we hold so dear.

Big-game taxidermy is a profession that preserves our attempts in the field—our memories of our successes and failures, as well as our hopes and dreams. You might not start out working on big-game animals—you might begin with upland birds or small game—but eventually, everyone in taxidermy ends up focusing on big game, at least for a time. In my first few attempts at big-game taxidermy, I created a few things that looked like they were—well, mildly deformed, and possibly mutant. Most folks don't get it right the first time. But the day I got it right made all of my early efforts worthwhile.

Webster's dictionary defines taxidermy as the skill or job of stuffing and mounting animal skins. The word *taxidermy* is constructed of two Latin roots: *taxi*, which means movement; and *derm*, which means skin. That's a pretty basic definition, referencing the removal and manipulation of an animal skin in preserving or mounting, and suggesting little about the artistic portion of the endeavor. But that's the trouble with language— one word can't describe everything. The same holds true with "fishing" or "hunting."

My goal with this book is threefold: to help the complete novice get started in big-game taxidermy; to help the amateur advance in talent; and to give the experienced taxidermist some useful insights. I cover the skinning, preserving, and mounting processes, and all the necessary finishing steps. I also address the essential mounts for any taxidermist: shoulder mounts for various deer, and European mounts and plaque mounts. Full-body mounts of mountain lions leaping onto the backs of black-tailed deer are for another book, one about advanced taxidermy work, so stay tuned—I'll write that one next.

Good luck, take your time, and enjoy it—and above all, feel free to be imaginative.

CHAPTER 1

Proper Field Care for a Trophy Mount

After greeting me at the door, my eager customer handed me his prize: a nice whitetail buck that had been skinned to the head before being removed from the rest of the carcass. The rack was very impressive, as very few deer from our part of North Carolina see a second birthday, much less the ripe old age of five, which this buck appeared to have reached. While I readied the paperwork, I listened in-

The author (left) on a New Mexico elk hunt.

tently to the hunter's tale of how events had unfolded on that dreary opening day.

All was fine until I took a closer look at the cape. It was extremely short with a large hole just under the throat patch. With a few questions I was able to gather enough information to find out what was up with the cape. The hunter had never taken a buck worthy of preserving for a lifetime of memories, nor had any of his hunting buddies, so without proper knowledge or research, the hunter had proceeded to cut the skin around the buck just forward of its shoulders. The end result was a cape that was approximately six inches or more too short for the common shoulder mount. And the unnecessary hole was due to a cut made to bleed the deer, a method passed down from one generation to another.

With a bit of advice, a skinning and field-care guide pamphlet in his pocket, and a bill for replacing the ruined cape, the hunter hopped in his truck and headed home. This hunter now knew how to handle a trophy buck in the future, but unfortunately, this same story plays out in taxidermy shops across the country several times each year.

Since I turned pro as a taxidermist, I have taken in some horrible cases of trophy animals that were supposed to be mounted, but very poor field care negated any attempt at making a quality mount. This really wasn't the hunter's fault, because often the fellow simply didn't understand the fragile nature of the bodies of these animals. Typical problems that occur include everything from fur loss due to dragging and skin slippage due to poor and lengthy storage, to the all-too-common short cape or cut throat. All of these situations are simply due to a lack of education.

Trophies subjected to these harsh conditions cause problems for the person appointed to re-create this piece of wildlife art. Many times the average hunter doesn't even give a second thought to the condition of their trophy as they leave it with the taxidermist. But they always seem to wonder why the same animal is less than perfect upon completion.

The best possible mount begins in the field with proper care of the trophy, and this should be planned well in advance of the hunt, before you shoot a trophy animal. Even highly skilled taxidermists can encounter complications which come from a poorly cared-for animal. And for those attempting to learn the skill of taxidermy on a less-than-perfect specimen, nothing short of a disaster is imminent. Nearing the halfway point of the mounting process only to have the hair begin slipping severely can be devastating for the novice taxidermist, and may be enough to frustrate him into quitting. Fortunately, taking proper precautions and knowing what to do in various situations can help reduce the risk of such an event.

Depending upon the circumstances of a hunt, you may suddenly find yourself with a trophy on your hands. But a little optimistic forethought doesn't hurt, especially if you know your chances of taking a big animal are good. Initially, the hunter should consider the pose he would like for the animal, as well as the positioning and eventual location of the mount. This is so the hunter can be extra cautious when dealing with certain areas of the animal. For example, if a life-size mount is chosen, then the entire skin should be closely cared for. But if a shoulder mount is the goal, obviously the head rearward to the shoulders is the only major concern. Also, many hunters may go for several seasons between trophies, so you've got to be extra careful about the one that you actually do get.

Even with proper knowledge and preparation, mishaps can take place. A couple years back a fellow went deer hunting in the suburbs of Virginia. Because of the location, only shotguns with buckshot were allowed. After a short sit in a tree, the hunter saw what appeared to be a trophy buck slowly walking in his direction. As the distance shortened to less than forty yards, the hunter readied his .12-gauge. At the blast the buck fell where it stood. Hurriedly, the hunter climbed to the ground to collect the largest buck he had ever had an opportunity to aim at. Upon nearing the buck he noticed the end of one antler was missing. "What happened?" the hunter thought. Further investigation revealed that apparently in the last millisecond, the deer had lowered his head and brought it rearward as if to lick or scratch. The buckshot had struck the trophy buck in the head, leaving numerous holes and a busted rack.

The hunter rushed home and called me, explaining the details of the morning's hunt. He asked if there was anything I could do to help. I told him to bring it over and we could discuss the situation. Before he arrived I was thinking of the options we might have should the skin and rack be damaged beyond repair—we could purchase another cape, or repair or cast the antlers. Nothing was certain until I saw the damage.

After discussing the options with the hunter, he clearly wanted to use as much of his buck as possible, even if it meant a less-than-perfect mount. I understood the distraught hunter's feelings all too well, so I diligently pieced the rack together and patched the numerous holes in the cape. The mount turned out okay, considering the circumstances, but it would have easily been a better mount with less work had this mishap not occurred. Now you may be thinking, "Well, heck, Triplett—accidents happen, and you shoot when you gotta shoot." Accidents certainly do happen, but thinking clearly when the moment of truth arrives will help matters exponentially. The quality of your trophy mount does, indeed, depend on your hunting skills—not just your ability to get a big, classic animal, but also to place your shot in such a way so that the taxidermist won't face major reconstruction.

Another hunter I know who faced a similar situation wasn't so lucky. While hunting for bear with hounds, he had the opportunity to take a large blackie that had bayed in an area with big boulders on three sides. In the past this hunter had encountered problems with injured bears inflicting serious wounds to his hounds after being shot. So instead of taking a body shot, which is always best in terms of repairs, he opted for a head shot in order to render the bear lifeless in an instant, thereby taking the heat off his dogs. The shot was well placed and everything went according to plan, until the hunter decided to have a life-size mount completed and found that the .300 Winchester Magnum had nearly torn the lower jaw from the bear. The damage was beyond repair, and only a bear rug was possible. Not bad, but not what he'd wanted.

In both of these cases, the hunters had plain old bad luck, which possibly could have been avoided with more forethought. Fortunately for the first hunter, the results of his bad luck could be repaired, but the roles could have easily been reversed. The lesson to be learned here is the importance of proper field care when it comes to trophy mounts.

There are three main rules to securing a quality big-game trophy:

- Avoid major damage to the skin, especially in the facial area.
- Keep the hair or fur free of any fluids (including water or bodily fluids).
- Cool the animal as soon as possible.

Avoiding skin damage can sometimes be tricky depending on the chosen weapon and the shot opportunity. An ideal caliber for most deer-sized game is the .270. A well-placed single shot from a .270 rifle is easily repairable. This also holds true for many larger calibers (my personal favorite is the 7mm Magnum), but don't opt for a neck shot with a .338 Winchester Magnum at an antelope that is slated for the wall. Additionally, bullet choice is critical. I have seen large-bore cartridges, up to the .338, produce moderate damage to even smallish deer. This is usually with a bullet that is designed for that animal—not too much, not too little. It seems that some bullets are built to inflict as much tissue damage as possible, which is fine for meat hunters or while hunting very large game, but for the mainstay of deer-sized animals, it can be too damaging.

Another key is keeping the hair and skin as dry as possible. While any bird or animal to be mounted will likely be washed at a later time, maintain a completely dry trophy in the field. Blood and most bodily fluids contain proteins that create stains, which are tough to remove completely without using chemicals or harsh washing. This seems to be especially true for antelope, Dall sheep, and mountain goats. Another disadvantage to soiling a skin with blood or water is that moisture makes up half of what is required for unwanted bacteria growth, with warmth serving as the other half of this damaging equation.

To avoid getting blood on the hair, take along paper towels, and after field dressing (or before transporting), clean the fur around the mouth and nose. If a life-size mount is the goal, clean around the bullet or arrow hole, and use paper towels to plug any wound that may seep significant amounts of blood onto the hair.

Of course, certain circumstances are unavoidable. If you happen to get caught in a pouring rain or an animal finds its way into a creek before expiring, the best thing to do is to skin the animal or cut the cape; remove the flesh; wash, then dry the pelt quickly, using compressed air; or, simply get the skin into a freezer immediately. If a freezer isn't handy, the next best thing is to dry the hair to the best of your ability without using a heat source, and then store it in a cool, dry place that will allow air to circulate around the skin. The best method for drying a trophy without the use of heat is to wipe the hair or fur with a cloth or paper towel, or if available, compressed air can help significantly. In a worst case scenario use your hands to wring excess water from the hair or fur.

This leads us to another key issue that has long been neglected by otherwise knowledgeable sportsmen: Getting your trophy to the freezer as quickly as possible should be a primary goal. Two main factors—the kind of critter taken, and the time of year—determine how quickly you must act before a trophy suffers severe damage. For example, a late-winter deer will be able to withstand a much greater delay in getting to cold storage than a late-summer or early-fall antelope. Some animal bodies, as you will soon learn, are able to endure heat more than others. But your best move is to get all animals skinned and frozen (or fleshed and salted) without hesitation.

Another serious mistake that haunts many hunters is their hauling a trophy around, showing it to friends. This problem doesn't seem as serious as it actually is. Hunters must understand that heat and moisture are prime breeding grounds for bacteria, which is enemy number-one to the taxidermist. And detrimental bacteria begin growing the moment an animal dies. Even an otherwise properly cared-for animal in nearly perfect condition can be lost due to slippage from bacteria buildup. Anyone can understand why a successful hunter wants to show

Quality big-game taxidermy begins in the field with the proper care of the quarry as soon as it is on the ground.

a trophy to their hunting buddies or co-workers, but this is a harmful delay to any game that is to be mounted. To avoid this problem and still be able to boast, take multiple quality photographs of your kill, go to a one-hour photo center if you're not shooting digital, and then pay a visit to everyone.

One more major rule to follow is to skip the field dressing if the mount desired will be life-size. By opening the animal in the field, more blood and fluids will be released, thus contaminating the fur. Just store the dead animal in a cold place as soon as possible, or go directly to the taxidermist.

Once these proper field-care guidelines have been followed, if you have time to start work immediately on the mount, do so. If not, proper storage at this point should be a priority. Initially, do not put the trophy into a plastic bag, as this will only retain heat and may create moisture if the animal is still warm. Place the animal into the freezer without a bag for at least an hour, then remove it and double-bag it to keep other freezer contaminants from getting on your prize. If freezer space is an issue, skin the body and then freeze the skin.

With all this completed, the stage is set to start work on creating your mount.

CHAPTER 2

The Essential Tools of Taxidermy

A s with any task, the outcome will be more desirable and the work more enjoyable if the right tools are available throughout the entire process. Some tools of the taxidermy trade can be rather pricey, but in the long run they are definitely worth the cost. In the initial learning stages, while all tools may not be an absolute must-have, possessing the best tools available will make certain tasks much simpler. What follows is a description of each implement needed, its uses, and, in my opinion, whether or not it is optional.

Latex Surgical Gloves

I have seen numerous taxidermists in my life who neglected the use of gloves of any kind while handling birds and mammals for mounts, saying they have a better touch on the subject without gloves. In my opinion, and that of others in the field who have seen firsthand the devastating effects of *not* wearing protective gear, going without gloves is asking for serious health problems caused by handling dead wild animals.

While most diseases that are prevalent in the animal kingdom can't be passed to humans, there are those which can. Rabies is probably at the top of the list, and although it usually isn't a problem with big game, other diseases do exist among

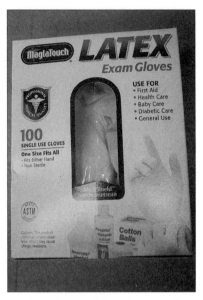

Save your hands by wearing latex gloves whenever you deal with chemicals, body fluids and parts, or when fleshing skins.

big game, including West Nile virus and anthrax. The chances of ever coming in contact with a bird or animal that has a transmittable disease is probably somewhere between slim and none, but once you contract one of these, you're stuck.

On the issue of gloves, the only question should be, "What size do I need?" This item is definitely *not* optional. For those who may be allergic to latex, other latex-free gloves are available. In my opinion they are suitable, but don't seem to be nearly as tough as gloves made from latex. Latex and latex alternative gloves can be purchased at most taxidermy suppliers, as well as drug stores.

Scalpel

This is probably the most important tool of the taxidermy trade, as it is used to skin all birds and mammals. And while many

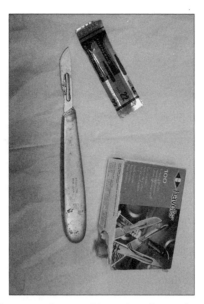

Keep your scalpels razor sharp—this makes for easier, smoother cutting and better work.

taxidermists might insist on a knife for skinning purposes, buying scalpels negates the need for regular sharpening, and they are relatively inexpensive when compared to the time it takes to sharpen a knife blade. Scalpels are also much sharper than any knife blade you could sharpen by hand.

Scalpels can be used alone, but are best suited for attachment to a scalpel handle. While small plastic scalpel handles are available, I advise you to invest a few extra dollars for a stainless-steel weighted handle. A weighted handle allows the scalpel to sit nicely in your hand while you work, and it will last a lifetime.

Be extra cautious when using scalpels. Even the poorest grade is razor sharp, and a careless slip can result in a serious cut. While scalpels are optional, in many cases they are much more effective than a knife.

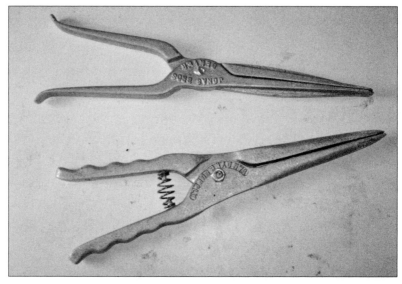

Ear openers are an indispensable tool in your effort to create a truly life-like mount, given the importance of ear detail.

Ear Openers

These are nearly priceless when turning the ear of most any animal, but especially one that may be exceptionally large. Instead of using a knife or scalpel to cut the attaching membrane between the skin and cartilage within the ear, you insert an ear opener carefully into the area between the ear butt and the surrounding skin, and gradually work it into the ear, toward the tip, until the ear is almost fully separated. This tool is similar in appearance to an extra long set of pliers, but instead of gripping, the opposing end pries the layers apart as the user squeezes the handle. For big-game animals, ear openers are a must.

Knives

Notice I said knives and not *knife*. While most beginners can start with one knife, a good supply of sharpened knives is ex-

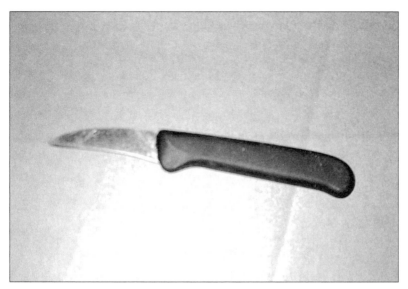

A short, strong blade, just like a hunting knife, is best for taxidermy work.

tremely beneficial to taxidermy work. Most of the work can be done with a supply of scalpels; however, there are body sections that might require a specialty knife, including thick skins, large areas that call for a longer blade, or heavily muscled parts. Selection largely depends on the particular animal at hand. Elk, buffalo, and several other large animals are especially hard on most any type of cutlery, as they usually dull a sharp edge more quickly than a light-skinned deer or antelope, so more frequent sharpening will be needed.

Different designs dot the market, but a good rule to keep in mind is to choose a blade in the three-inch range that is easily sharpened and maintains its sharpness. You'll also need a knife with some serious backbone for heavier animals. And remember that the adage "You get what you pay for" applies completely to knives. A good skinner or hunting knife might cost around $140, but it will last for a long time. Consider at least one knife to be a mandatory part of your collection.

Scissors

Small, curved scissors can be used to trim around bullet holes or to reach otherwise inaccessible areas, such as the base of the tail or inside the paws. These small, inexpensive scissors can be priceless when dealing with fat or muscle tissue that is very thin and holding tight against the skin. Quality surgical scissors of various sizes are the way to go. Scissors made specifically for taxidermy can only be acquired from a taxidermy supplier, as those available from general retailers aren't designed for thick skin. Scissors are optional but highly valuable.

Sculpting Tool

A sculpting tool lends itself to many uses. Placing epoxies into shrunken areas, shaping the area around each eye, and shaping the interior of each nostril during the mounting process are all things that can be done with a sculpting tool. Though a Dremel tool is very handy for obtaining a quick, general shape of the interior of the nostril, entire shaping of the nostril opening can be made using a sculpting tool alone. You will probably find many other uses for this must-have implement. Sculpting tools

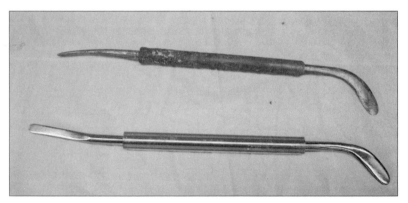

Consider the sculpting tool your paintbrush.

are made of plastic, wood, and stainless steel, and can be purchased at Research Mannikins. Another great trick is to shape the wooden end of a paintbrush to a flat angle by using a knife to create a shape similar to that of narrow flathead screwdriver tip. This allows the taxidermist to shape with one end and clean up and blend with the other. I recommend the stainless-steel version, but if possible, obtain a few different designs and materials, as different designs will lend themselves well to individual tasks. A sculpting tool of some kind, whether homemade or a commercial tool is an absolute necessity for producing a quality mount.

Note: I use the term *manikin* in this book to designate the manufactured armature on which you mount a skin. You might see this word spelled as *mannikin* in some places (an alternate spelling). A *mannequin* is that plastic statue thing you see wearing ladies' clothing in the department store window.

Skin Stretchers

A skin stretcher can be used for pulling a skin into position on a manikin. It is also very beneficial, if not mandatory, for stretching a rug. Skin stretchers look very much like heavy-duty pliers, with a very wide grip for securing skins without tearing them and providing a firm grip to pull the edges of skin into position for either sewing or stapling. Skin stretchers are so helpful with some jobs that they verge on being mandatory.

Fleshing Machine

While beginners can flesh most big-game animals slated for a shoulder mount with a knife, scalpel, scissors, and a fleshing beam—which is simply a narrow beam approximately six inches across that is used to lay the skin across, hair side down, while flesh is removed from the skin side using a fleshing tool

A rotary-blade flesher spins a metal disk with a curved outer edge that strips excess flesh away from a skin.

or knife—better and quicker results can be achieved by using a fleshing machine. Two different types of fleshing machines are available.

The first type is a *small-game* or *bird flesher*, which utilizes a wire wheel that attaches directly to a small electric motor, usually less than one horsepower. The mechanics are similar to the brush side of a bench grinder, except that the small-game flesher incorporates side shields. These shields are in place to prevent any flesh particles from littering the user or the work area. This type of fleshing machine is workable for small deer and other species when the bulk of the flesh has already been removed and all that is needed is minor dressing up of the skin.

The upside of this type of flesher is that it rarely cuts a hole in the skin, and it is very inexpensive. The downside is that the small-game flesher isn't nearly as effective as a rotary knife for fleshing. It can also heat the skin with friction, thus potentially creating ideal conditions for bacteria growth.

The second—and most preferred type of fleshing machine for big game—is referred to as a *rotary-blade flesher* or *rotary knife*. This is composed of a round metal disc or "blade," ten to fifteen inches in diameter, which has been sharpened around the edge, with the outermost eighth of an inch along the entire circumference bent to form a 90-degree angle. This allows the user to pull the skin from left to right across the blade as it turns, cutting any excess tissue from the skin. The rotary fleshing machine is generally better suited for deer-sized species and larger, but can be useful on even the smallest mammals if used properly.

If a serious attempt at taxidermy is your goal, purchase a rotary flesher. A flesher will likely be the largest investment you make during the initial stages of taxidermy. However, once the initial investment is made—usually around $1,000—a quality flesher will quickly pay for itself in the reduction of time spent properly fleshing a skin.

Fortunately, in recent years several companies have began making fleshers, and you can find some units for under $1,000. But as with anything, lower price can often mean lower quality, so be careful with your selection. Research Mannikins sells the Advanced Fleshing Machine, and although it is a bit more costly, at approximately $1,450, it could possibly be one of the best fleshers available, lasting the user a lifetime.

One other great alternative to finding a quality flesher is to visit an Internet taxidermy forum or a hands-on taxidermy class to locate a used one. A high-quality flesher is nearly impossible to damage through normal use, so a used model can sometimes be as good or better, cost-wise, than a new model.

Some may consider the rotary flesher optional, and fleshing can certainly be performed with a standard knife and scissors, but I recommend putting the rotary flesher or knife high on the must-have list.

Bondo

It might seem strange to see a substance that is usually classified as an automotive supply in a taxidermy tools list, but the fact is that without Bondo, the taxidermy world would be scrambling to find an exact substitute. Bondo has many appli-

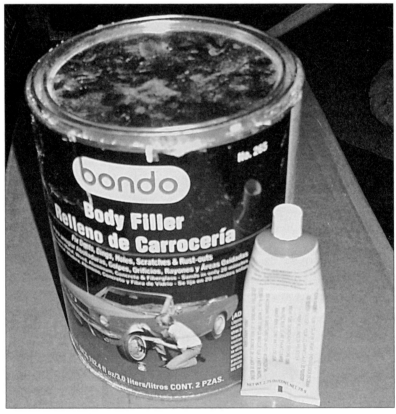

In the same way you use Bondo on a car, you can use it to fill gaps and create body contours on an animal mount.

cations in the taxidermy shop: manikin repair; quickly setting the base of a spread turkey tail; attaching artificial fish heads; and serving as a base for antlers or horns on big-game manikins, among multiple other uses. When purchasing Bondo, no special formulation is needed—you can purchase whatever kind is available at your local convenience or automotive store.

Nearly all life-size manikins and many large-shouldered manikins for elk, buffalo, and other sizeable game are cut into two or more pieces for ease of shipping. After these manikins arrive, they must be put back together, and Bondo, along with an ample amount of hardener, is the necessary ingredient here.

Clay

Clay is a mainstay of taxidermy work. It is used to sculpt around eyes, fill in imperfections in the manikin, fill in and re-sculpt around horn and antler skull caps and to transition between toes, hooves, and the leg ends of most manikins.

The uses of clay for taxidermy are endless and it is an absolute necessity. For cost savings, I recommend using Critter Clay, which exhibits much less shrinkage than regular clay, for sculpting highly detailed areas such as around the eyes, and bulk clay for filling in depressions, ear bases, and filling in around the skull plate.

Wire

Taxidermy of small game and birds requires an abundance of wire. But for the big-game taxidermist, wire is generally reserved only for the tails of life-size mounts and for helping to hold the ears in a desired position during the drying stage. Wire can also be used to help mend damaged or intentionally altered manikins. Various sizes are available through Research Mannikins at a fairly inexpensive price. Start out with a small portion of each gauge (from 8- to 16-gauge) in order to determine what you use most.

Manikins

Prior to the early 1980s, many taxidermists would clean the skull of the specimen they intended to mount; then, they would add clay to form the muscles around the head, giving it the correct shape. If the taxidermist was mounting a life-size piece, he would turn his attention to shaping the body by forming a wooden frame and then adding excelsior to form the muscle groups. Once he had a generic shape, he would wrap twine around the mass to help hold it together. This technique was crude, to say the least, but it was the most common procedure at the time.

Some of the best taxidermists in the country would build the skeletal structure from wood and wire and then cover it

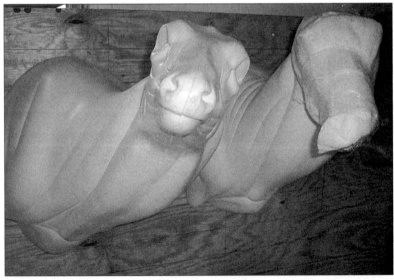

The development of animal manikins for taxidermy presents a great advantage over the old skull-and-wood-frame methods.

with clay, sculpting the desired shape. This was the most time-consuming, but the most accurate.

Of course, taxidermy evolved over the years, and top taxidermists in the country began to study mammal anatomy and physiology more closely. After casting, measuring, and studying thousands of specimens, taxidermists slowly began to produce more anatomically accurate animal bodies. Today's manikins are made of hard foam that is easily altered if the need arises, and most are highly detailed for a convincing appearance once they are completed.

You can also find contemporary manikins in virtually every desired realistic position—sitting, leaping, and turning, to name a few. And if the perfect size can't be found, most can be easily altered. At times a commercially produced manikin can be modified to accommodate an animal that is very rarely mounted; a taxidermist simply has to use his imagination. I recently had the opportunity to work on a bobcat attacking a piglet. This was a commercial piece, and because of financial barriers the customer didn't want to do a carcass cast, which involves skinning an animal, casting the carcass, and then creating a matching manikin. So before I decided I'd have to beg off the project, I did a bit of research. I found a javelina manikin that was about five inches too long and two inches too large in girth. After several cuts and reconnections, cutting the head down and sanding along with a few test fits, the commercially made javelina manikin filled in for the piglet very well. It pays to be creative.

Eyes

The eyes can make or break a mount. You can put together a mount very well, but if you use a poor grade of eye, the living look that all taxidermists strive for suffers as a result. On the flip side, an average mount with a high-quality eye can look

Choose carefully the eyes for your mounts, and be willing to spend on quality, as these are a crucial detail.

great. People are visual creatures, and eye contact is very important. Even someone who is not knowledgeable about taxidermy will notice the eyes first. Thus, installing top-quality eyes can lock in that good first impression, especially when someone is paying you a good deal of money to give them the trophy of a lifetime.

The artificial eye has come a long a way in the past twenty years. (That's a statement you'd read only in a taxidermy book, isn't it?) In the late 1970s and early 1980s, most eyes looked more like glass balls that had been cut in half. But today, most eye companies produce at least one series of eyes that incorporates a correct shape (an eyeball isn't completely round), with a true-to-life color. Budgets are always tight, but if you're going to spend, spend on the eyes.

Adhesive

Adhesive serves two purposes: (1) It allows the skin to be easily moved about the manikin with little resistance; and (2) Once dry, it will attach the skin firmly to the manikin, prohibiting it from *drumming*—a drumlike effect similar to placing a skin over the head of a drum. It occurs when the skin dries and pulls away from any low spot on the manikin, thus creating an area where the skin doesn't adhere, and a hollow space between the skin and the manikin remains.

Different types of adhesives are available. One of the oldest forms is a *dextrin-based adhesive*. The advantage of a dextrin adhesive is the fact that it can take up to a couple of days to dry. This allows the taxidermist time to make any necessary last-minute adjustments. On the other hand, if the skin begins to dry and shrink before the adhesive sets properly, the skin might drum. Nonetheless, many veteran taxidermists swear by a dextrin-based glue, and it definitely has a permanent place in taxidermy.

Another adhesive that is relatively new to the field is an *epoxy adhesive*, which consists of two parts that must be mixed thoroughly together before hardening occurs. Epoxy adhesives are advantageous because most will adhere and harden within two to three hours. This allows the skin to be locked down before it begins to dry, alleviating any drumming. The drawback of using an epoxy as opposed to dextrin-based glue is that your working time is greatly decreased.

I strongly recommend that those who are still in the taxidermy learning process avoid an epoxy-based adhesive, because initially, mistakes will be made, and an epoxy allows very little time or chance for correction. As you gather experience, you can decide to switch to an epoxy-based adhesive. One trick used by many taxidermists that you can follow is to apply epoxy-based adhesive to the facial areas, as these areas are usually not disposed to drumming, and then use dextrin-based adhesive on the remainder of the body.

Degreaser

Proper degreasing is very important—practically mandatory—when dealing with any fatty animal such as a bear or wild hog, but a quality degreaser will be beneficial when dealing with most any animal skin. Bear skins are extremely greasy, and, in my opinion, only a commercial tannery can deal with them properly, as a commercial outfit is better equipped to handle degreasing chores. Commercial degreasing vats are large and their contents are consistently monitored to achieve a premium product.

Several methods exist for basic cleaning and degreasing. Many top taxidermists in the country swear by Dawn dishwashing liquid, saying that it is their only degreaser. I have used Dawn in the past, but now I prefer to use it in conjunction with a commercial degreaser. With a commercial degreaser, I have found that my skins come out shinier and cleaner, thus producing a superior mount; in my opinion, total degreasing is a must for a quality mount.

Dry Preservative or Tan

Most beginners that try taxidermy start with a dry preservative, and some even begin with "20-Mule Team" Borax, which is available at most grocery stores. Borax generally works well on small game, but for big game, specially formulated dry preservatives tend to work best. The primary purpose of dry preservative is to remove moisture and to help bug-proof the skin. Differing opinions abound on the adequacy of dry preservative. For my own work, I feel that a quality dry preservative is fine for animals up to deer-sized game, while larger big-game animals are better off being tanned.

Numerous tans that work well are available at most taxidermy suppliers. Also, there is the highly advised option of using a commercial tannery. While all who want to truly learn the art of taxidermy should eventually master the tanning process, a quality commercial tanner is preferred for most larger animals. This is especially true when dealing with greasy or extremely dirty animals (feral hogs probably top the greasy-and-dirty list). The tanning process will be explained in more detail in chapter 6.

Tumbler

This is also one of the highest-priced tools on the supply list, and, thankfully, the one that is the most optional. Don't misunderstand "optional" as meaning "totally unnecessary." A tumbler is a definite asset, and while the art of taxidermy can be performed without one, it is a very helpful tool. A tumbler is a 30–50 gallon barrel that is placed sideways on framework; it is then turned by a small electric motor of approximately 1 hp. The tumbler is a definite time-saver. Wet skins can be deposited into a tumbler and after a short cycle, come out virtually dry with only a slight touch-up needed before continuing the mounting procedure. The action of the tumbler also helps to reduce any unwanted oils and enhance the hair's luster. There are, however, taxidermists with years of experience that choose not to tumble their skins.

Tumblers can be used in conjunction with various contents, but corncob grit and hardwood sawdust are probably the most

Tumblers can greatly speed up the drying process for a pelt, but they are not totally necessary if you've got time.

popular. Corncob grit comes in two sizes, coarse and fine; the size you choose is based on your personal preference. Most taxidermists prefer the coarse corncob grit for mammal work, but some choose the fine, with a mix of the two offering a quality medium. The tumbler is filled from one-third to almost half full with this tumbling mix. Many taxidermists like to add various ingredients to their corncob grit or hardwood sawdust, including odorless mineral spirits, dry preservative, hair sheen, or a mixture of the above. Tumblers work well for the cleaning and drying of most any mammal skins, so if you plan to make taxidermy a longtime hobby or a career, then the tumbler is definitely a good investment. The price for a quality tumbler ranges from $300-$600, depending on the size of the barrel and the individual manufacturer.

Stout Ruffer

When manikins are manufactured, a thin layer remains on the surface that is impervious to adhesion. This is caused by the release agent used to keep the manikin from sticking to the mold. To enable the skin to adhere to the manikin, this outer layer must be removed. This is done with one of the tools available to rough the surface of the manikin. While several different tools are available, many prefer the Stout Ruffer, sold by Research Mannikins. Use this tool to scrape the outer slick layer of foam from the manikin before applying adhesive; then, you can proceed when you're ready. A Stout Ruffer is also very useful in positioning the skin during the mounting process. A ruffer is optional, but a tool that roughs the surface of a manikin is necessary, and the Stout Ruffer fills this need well.

Regulator Needles

Regulator needles come in various lengths, but both the long and short versions work very well. These needles are very useful for

You can hold the skin in place for sewing quite easily with a dozen or so regulator needles.

positioning the skin, holding the skin in position while sewing incisions, and generally moving the skin around and into basic positions. Regulators are inexpensive, so you may want to buy several. While this tool is optional, it is quite beneficial.

Airbrush

When it comes to preservation methods in the taxidermy industry, tremendous strides have been made in recent years. The same holds true with the painting techniques used to add

Careful airbrushing is crucial to facial details, but calls for painting talent.

natural color to the finished product—the step that truly brings the mount to life.

Not so long ago, painting techniques involved the use of paintbrushes and automotive lacquers or oil paints. The end result was usually suitable when delivered by the highly skilled, but most often it was less than desirable when the product of a beginner. Oftentimes those first attempts with the older coloring methods caused great frustration among beginners, making them doubt their ability to reach higher levels of preservation.

When taxidermists first chose to attempt the use of an airbrush, probably sometime in the 1980s, they were able to perform fantastic work. About the time the airbrush was introduced to the art of taxidermy, production companies also redefined the paints that were used. Instead of borrowing paints from other trades, someone decided it was time to specially formulate paints just for wildlife artistry. For the experienced taxidermist, these customized colors can produce an incredible finished product. And for those just learning, airbrushing with these new paints might shave months, if not years, from the time needed to create great results.

Many highly respected individuals in the taxidermy field remain devoted to the traditional paintbrush and oil paints, but those who prefer this older method are small in number. And while the airbrush is an optional tool, it is more than worth the minimal investment. For big game taxidermy an airbrush of approximately forty dollars will be suitable, no matter the brand. An assortment of airbrushes can be found at Research Mannikins.

WHERE TO SHOP

A list of suppliers can be found in the Appendix, beginning on page 209. I've worked with Research Mannikins for a number of years, and find their materials and service to be as good as any you can find. When you first start out, or when money is tight, you might be able to find secondhand supplies and tools for sale online or at taxidermy shows. Getting in touch with a taxidermists' association is also a good way to find quality used supplies. To locate a state or local taxidermist's association on the Internet, simply type in the state in which you reside followed by the words "taxidermist association" and this should quickly put you in touch with a state organization. If Internet service isn't available, or should you have problems finding a local taxidermist organization, contact Research Mannikins; they have a list of almost every taxidermist association within the country.

CHAPTER 3

Reference and Anatomy for Big-Game Taxidermy

A s I have explained in my four previous books on taxidermy, I have always been fascinated by wildlife artwork created by human hands. I used to think there was some kind of secret or magic to drawing, sculpture, and taxidermy. On a trip to Yellowstone National Park as a teenager, I watched a painter in one of the information centers creating an exceptional portrait of a buffalo. I thought maybe the guy was just going on pure memory, but then I noticed that he often peered through a small eyepiece on his workbench. When I asked him what he was looking at, he graciously allowed me to have a look too. Through the small eyepiece I could see a photograph of a life-size buffalo, identical to the one being painted. The man explained that all artists use reference material to duplicate the anatomy, size, and other important features of their intended work. This was an important lesson for me about how wildlife art is created, and one that I could apply as a taxidermist.

The best wildlife artists in the world, including taxidermists, constantly study and observe the species they intend to recreate. Even those taxidermists who have created mounts of innumerable species continue to observe such creatures in the wild, as well as studying the bodies of animals obtained by hunters, and watching animals in zoos and preserves. I would go so far as to say that you probably can't make any decent animal mounts until you have become highly familiar with those species you prefer to work on. Knowing just how a turkey struts or how a deer raises its head can make all the difference when it comes to the liveliness and accuracy of the mounts you create.

REFERENCE MATERIAL

You can study photos, videos, and paintings, which are considered *two-dimensional references*. Live specimens and death masks are *three-dimensional references*. All reference is valuable when preparing to create a mount. It is also best not to rely on just one form of reference.

Reference material should encompass all periods of an animal's life, like this bull elk in velvet.

A word of caution here: Don't consider other taxidermists' mounted animals as true references. I do highly recommend observing other taxidermists' efforts, as this can help with improving your own technique. But a mount is the taxidermist's interpretation of what a creature should look like, and isn't necessarily 100 percent accurate, like an image of a live animal would be. It is merely an individualized perception of that creature, making a live animal your best reference.

In an ideal situation the taxidermist would have ready access to an animal pen or a pet for reference study. Most award-winning taxidermists use live animals consistently as reference. While some states allow the ownership of certain wildlife, be careful should you choose this method. First, check state laws, as there are restrictions on the ownership of most wild animals. Then, learn as much as possible about the animal. This will help alleviate any future problems you may encounter with the particular animal. Care, feeding, environmental needs, and

Observe live any animal species that you can—some are easier to find than others, such as bison at zoos.

health care should be primary concerns. Deer are probably the most common live reference source, as they are the easiest to obtain and aren't as problematic as other big-game animals.

If animal ownership is out of the question, other viable options remain. A library of videos is a great resource. Most hunting videos captivate their audiences by showing animals as they cautiously make their way to the hunter. It is fairly easy to obtain footage of most any animal, and although close-up footage may be limited, a taxidermist can get quality reference for body posture and individual attitude. In addition, you may visit a zoo or national park with a personal camcorder. The footage collected may prove to be priceless. If the primary focus is deer, most national parks are full of opportunity. A good number of deer in a park environment may come within a few feet of you, as they are never hunted and therefore aren't very fearful, so quality close-ups should be easily achieved.

Two-dimensional reference materials are probably some of the cheapest and easiest we can acquire, and with big game, they are a viable solution. If you want to mount your own deer or other big game, it's likely you are a hunter—and I don't know of any hunter who doesn't have numerous hunting videos and stacks of magazines lying around the house. Most of these magazines and videos are full of live footage or photos of an assortment of big-game animals. Obtaining these sources of reference will provide a double return on any investment. You will not only enjoy the good reading and entertainment value, but you will also have the opportunity to study an endless array of wildlife photos in preparation for future taxidermy projects.

If you desire closer shots or more precise pictures, a full selection is available through most taxidermy suppliers. These photos will have high-quality close-ups of specific areas on the animals. Angles and positioning of ears, nose, eyes, and mouth are easily studied with these area-specific photos. I highly recommend getting at least one booklet from a quali-

Take note of how a given species moves and stands, and try to translate that into your mounts.

fied reference photographer, as well as all the other free photos you can acquire.

An ideal way to begin a reference library is to get several folders and label them with potential reference contents, one folder for each species—deer, bear, boar, and so forth. Once a hunting magazine is retired, sift through it and cut out the photos that you need. These photos are great for studying poses and body positions. This will serve two purposes: It will offer you lifelong reference material, and it will also make amends with a spouse who can't understand why so many magazines are just lying around.

Additional reference can be gained from your own outdoor and hunting experiences. Every excursion into the field, whether during a specific season or any other time, is a chance to watch how animals move, stand, and react to stimuli. Once you familiarize yourself with what to look for, you will notice an amazing array of details.

Keep watch while you hunt—you might observe animal movements, like that of this doe, that are useful reference.

One unique three-dimensional reference is the *death mask*, which is a reproduction of a particular part of chosen anatomy. For example, death masks are readily made of big-game noses, eyes (the entire area around the eye), and even entire animal heads or facial features. These death masks are made shortly after an animal's death; hence, the name. (Human death masks are almost always molds taken of the deceased person's face shortly after death.) These are made by pouring a molding material—latex is preferred by many, but other materials are available—onto a desired subject. Then, plaster is usually poured onto the latex to act as a mother mold. Once dry, the mold is cut in half and removed from the animal, and then the mold is rejoined and a material suitable for casting is poured into it. This forms a three-dimensional impression with depth, distance, and angles that can't be studied using photos. Making these casts is an advanced procedure, and I won't go into detail about it here. But numerous commercial casts of almost any mountable animal are available. Also, several quality videos and books devoted solely to molding and casting are available through most taxidermy suppliers.

After some compilation of reference materials, you will be ready to start learning how to read them and better understand how they can help you to create lifelike mounts. For instance, if you show a picture of a bedded, very drowsy-looking deer to an individual untrained in reading animal reference and ask him what he sees, he will likely say, "I see a deer." Although this statement isn't totally wrong, it isn't the answer that a taxidermist would give. Ask the same question of one trained to view and understand reference, and they will likely respond with comments about the apparent attitude of the deer—how it appears sleepy, or very relaxed. This trained observer will also comment on the position of the legs, head, tail, and ears. This kind of detail-mindedness is what the budding taxidermist must develop, because all of these finer points go into the process of making a mount look truly lifelike.

Test how good an observer you are by watching a live animal and noting how many of its details change as you watch.

To do a competent job as a taxidermist, you must break down a picture while studying it. Instead of looking at a picture as a whole, you must learn to notice each particular detail of your study piece. An excellent way to learn this is to apply straight lines within a photo to better understand angles and shapes that are pertinent to the re-creation of a subject. I have found a good study tool to be a piece of paper with a small, box-shaped hole cut in the center of it. The size of the box will depend on the size of the photo you are working with; the smaller the photo, the smaller the box.

To use this tool, place a picture of a deer on a surface in front of you, and by using the small box, isolate an individual area that you would like to learn more about. For example, focus on the head area, because that is one of the most prominent features in any mount, but especially in a shoulder mount. Box off the eye and place a ruler or any straight-edged object horizontally or vertically across the opening in the box. You will quickly notice angles and shapes that were previously overlooked. This will help you when it comes to the proper positioning of the skin as it should fit around the eye. You will quickly see that the eye isn't round, as many think; rather, it is an angled oval shape. Also, eye shape is heavily dictated by mood. A frightened or excited animal will have a wider eye, while the eyes of a relaxed animal will be much more squinted. Another example might be to box off the ears of an alert or even aggressive deer, or other big-game animal. You should immediately notice that the angle at which the ears flow into the head varies a great deal depending on mood. By using the straightedge, you will get a better understanding of how and where body parts should join. The uses of this cutout are limitless and can be very beneficial to the learning process.

Your goal in making a mount should be to re-create the animal as perfectly as possible—that is to say, if someone looked at the mount, they'd swear it was alive. The more you work,

Animal reactions, like that of this antelope at attention, its mouth open, also play a big role in quality taxidermy.

the better you will get at using reference to refine your mounts, and the better you get at making mounts, the better your understanding will be of how to use, interpret, and implement the many details of reference materials. When this begins to happen, you will understand how taxidermy is truly an art form, and you're the artist.

ANATOMY

The definition of *anatomy*, for our purposes, is the physical structure of an animal, and in big-game taxidermy, this involves both the muscular and skeletal structure of a given mammal. You might think that anatomy is best left to the sculptors who spend countless hours studying and reproducing animals in the form of manikins. Indeed, much of the skeletal and muscular reproduction is inherent in today's modern manikins. However, learning as much as possible about animals' bodies will help you to reconstruct them more naturally, and will allow you to customize a manikin, or correct the occasional flaws that sometimes occur in manikins.

Understanding anatomy also prevents you from making small errors in constructing a mount that can add up to an inaccurate overall look for a given animal. Say you mounted a life-size bear with its ears sticking straight out and its forelegs locked in an unnatural stance. Just those two anatomical inaccuracies alone would cancel out the ultimate effect of all your work. You might not make a huge mistake anywhere, but without a better understanding of anatomy, you could complete a project that is still anatomically incorrect.

True—the manikins produced for big game already include the shoulders, neck, and head for shoulder mounts, and the body and legs for life-size mounts; the physical structure is already there for you to work with. I wouldn't take this advantage for granted, however. I urge you to keep up your anatomical studies of any species you might mount.

Anatomy isn't one of those subjects that you can fully learn and understand in just a few paragraphs, or a few hours. Learning it really never ends. On the bright side, if you understand the basics, you will continue to learn as you do more research and tackle more projects. An excellent way to learn more about anatomy is to pay attention during the skinning process. By working with a specimen before skinning begins, you can get a better understanding of that species. Before any skinning takes place, it is easy to swivel and bend an animal's legs, head, and other moveable parts so you can at least get an idea about the creature's range of motion. Before a deer or bear is skinned, you will find that you cannot bend a leg very far in any direction before a ligament or muscle group stops this movement. This helps you to understand that if you mounted the animal with its leg or head in such an overextended position, it would appear wholly unnatural.

Also, while skinning an animal, take notice of how each bone is attached to the next, as well as how the muscles attach and hold the bones. This kind of learning occurs with every project. Even today, I will learn something new while skinning an animal. By making mental notes of how all the parts go together, you will quickly begin to understand what is natural and what isn't. And that is what taxidermy is all about—natural duplication.

CHAPTER 4

Skinning Big-Game Animals

C omparatively speaking, proper skinning and thorough fleshing of a given animal is just as important as the mounting procedure. Although the mounting phase is the point at which the appearance is finalized and the mount comes to life, without proper skinning and fleshing, a lifelike appearance will be difficult to achieve. In addition, the longevity of the mount may suffer.

Put another way, painting and siding might be what give a house its attractive appearance, but without a properly configured frame and trim placement, the structure will weather quickly and will ultimately be weak, even though it appears to be sound. The same goes for taxidermy. Skinning and fleshing create the foundation and underlying strength of your mount.

These procedures may seem difficult at first, but like many other steps in taxidermy, they will quickly become second nature. Until you have reached a point where an animal can be skinned with relative ease, you should practice as much as possible. Practice is best performed on animals that aren't slated for mounting, or ones that aren't unique or special. During the initial learning stages mistakes will be made, and these mistakes are much easier to absorb on a critter that isn't highly valuable as a taxidermy specimen.

OBTAINING PROPER MEASUREMENTS

Before and after the skinning process takes place, you must obtain and record some measurements. Measurements are of utmost importance, because while performing taxidermy, you should put no more into the skin than is taken out. Imagine a balloon that is designed to hold one gallon of water. The balloon represents the skin of an animal, and the gallon of water is the muscular and skeletal structure. During the skinning procedure, you are removing the carcass from within the skin. This is similar to removing the water from the balloon. Once the carcass is removed from the skin, the taxidermist will replace the biodegradable carcass with a synthetic carcass, which in turn provides the desired shape of the species on hand. However, if the taxidermist uses a manikin that is much (or even slightly) too large for the skin, this would be like placing more than a gallon of water back into the balloon. The end result would either be severe stretching or tearing of the balloon or skin. At best, the mounting process would be very difficult and time-consuming to complete. At worst, the skin could be damaged beyond repair, or the skin of the mount could shift considerably after drying, leaving a virtual mess.

To alleviate these problems, take your body measurements from the actual carcass. Some taxidermists rely on the measurements of the skin once it has been removed from the carcass, but these measurements can be misleading. To get a good idea of how this method can be skewed, grab a dog by the skin of its back and give a lift; you will immediately notice all of the extra skin. By doing this, it is easy to see that raw skin can stretch tremendously. In some situations, you may not have the luxury of measuring the carcass; for example, when a hunter has already done the skinning. In this case, measure the skin without overly stretching it, as this will provide a much more accurate measurement than if you stretched the skin tight and then took the measurements.

The eye-to-nose measurement should be obtained prior to the skinning process. This is done by using calipers, which are available from most taxidermy suppliers. To obtain an accurate measurement, place one tip of the calipers on the center of the nose, and then open the calipers until the opposite point rests in the corner of an eye. Then, with a ruler, measure the distance between the two points. In a pinch these measurements can be taken by stretching a tape measure between the tip of the nose and front corner of the eye, then subtracting a quarter of an inch. Using calipers is simply more exact.

If the desired mount is to be life-size, one more measurement can be taken before skinning, and this is the length from the tip of the nose to the base of the tail. To obtain an accurate measurement, place the animal in a pose similar to the one chosen for mounting. Then, hold a flexible measuring tape to the tip of the nose; while holding it against the curvature of the body (along the top of the skull and along the spine), extend it to the base of the tail, or to where the tail begins to protrude from the body. This should produce an accurate length measurement.

Other measurements should be taken after the skinning process is complete. Most important for life-size mounts is the girth, but other important measurements for a shoulder mount include the neck girth, and the length and width of the head. These head and neck measurements are also beneficial for life-size mounts. The girth of the body as well as the neck should be measured after skinning, because if the measurement is taken over the top of the skin and hair or fur, this may distort the results by up to a couple of inches. There are some who measure the girth prior to skinning and then estimate by subtracting a small amount, depending on the particular animal, from the total. While this will usually be close enough, it isn't always exact.

For measurements when a carcass isn't available, the taxidermist must resort to skin measurements, estimations, and experience. If, for example, you were to purchase a skin for taxidermy purposes, it may have already been tanned. Sometimes these skins will be accompanied by measurements, but other times you won't be that lucky.

To measure a skin without the carcass, spread it out evenly and uniformly without stretching it. After recording the measurements of the skin only and referring to a supply catalog for a manikin, you might find that your recorded length is two inches too long, while the girth is an inch too short. This is where experience is helpful, but even the beginner can sift through the available sizes and choose a manikin that is most appropriate. Just remember, most often, choosing a manikin that is too small rather than too large will be a tremendous help during the mounting process. The skin could easily have been stretched in length, which would decrease the girth measurement; therefore, I would order the closest-sized manikin possible and begin test-fitting. If this method is used when choosing a manikin, the skin should fit without too much difficulty.

Most taxidermy suppliers use the same kind of body measurements that I've just described. For shoulder manikins, these include a measurement around the small of the neck at the head-neck junction, and then across the atlas of the neck—which is tight under the lower jaw, but four inches down the back of the neck. All taxidermy supply catalogs visibly show the corresponding measurement areas, and some will differ slightly from one to another. Most of these measurements are illustrated in individual taxidermy supply manuals. Other measurements listed by taxidermy suppliers will include an eye-to-nose measurement (pertinent to all manikins), a length measurement (taken from the base of the tail to the tip of the nose), and a girth measurement (taken at the largest point of the midsection). Some companies even include a neck girth and a measurement from the front of the nose to the back of the head for life-size manikins. Even if the supplier you choose doesn't include these extra measurements, you should record them, because this will ensure proper fit and a good guideline for cross-reference should any manikin alterations be attempted.

SKINNING METHODS

After you've taken most measurements, the skinning process can begin. The mount desired will dictate the skinning method chosen.

Shoulder-Mount Skinning

When mounting big game, the shoulder mount is easily more popular than a life-size mount, as a life-size deer, elk, or even antelope can take up a lot of space in the living room, and full-body mounts are exponentially higher in price. For the shoulder mount, many skinning methods are available. There are *full-length* and *short Y-, V-, T-, and 7-cuts* for horned or antlered animals. Each is named after the shape of the cuts from antler to antler across the back of the head. In addition, when mounting bear, boar, or any animal that does not have horns, you will want to skin without making any incision up the back of the neck and head. Choosing which incision to use is largely based on personal preference, but is also influenced by the length of the hair on the animal being mounted, the chosen pose, or whether or not you are making a competition piece. Probably the most popular is the full-length or short Y-cut, discussed later in this section.

Most beginning big-game taxidermists will very likely start with a shoulder mount of a deer, which is easily the most

When cutting for a shoulder mount, cut well behind the shoulders and just above the first joint of the leg—every inch of skin is crucial for fit.

accessible big-game animal. Skinning for a shoulder mount is relatively easy with some practice, but if skinning procedures aren't completed according to the following guidelines, problems can occur. Most problems in shoulder mounts arise from having a skin that is too short in length, or the front legs have been cut off too close to the body, creating a cape that is too short in the armpit area.

A good guideline to follow, when in doubt, is to leave excessive skin when skinning for a shoulder mount. Thus, you should make the initial cut around the body of the animal, approximately halfway between the shoulders and the hips, and cut the skin around the knee of each leg. Remember—excess skin can be cut off *after* the mounting process is complete, but it can't be reattached. Well, actually, skin *can* be reattached if it is available, but doing so creates more work for the taxidermist, along with the fact that the finished product is inferior.

Full-length and Short Y-, V-, T-, and 7-Cuts

All of these incisions are somewhat similar; their only true difference is the shape of the incision on the back of the head,
which is made to free the skin around the antlers or horns.
Generally, the V- and 7-incisions are reserved for competition
pieces, but some taxidermists have figured out how to incorpo-
rate these cuts into their commercial mounts without too much
hassle. The V- and 7-cuts make for less sewing and shorter
seams, and these factors, in my opinion, provide a better finished product. On the downside, fleshing and test-fitting can be
more time-consuming than when using a full-length Y-cut,
which provides a flat skin. A good method to begin with is
probably the short Y. It allows more room to maneuver the
head while skinning, but because the incision only goes three
to five inches down the back of the neck from the V-cut, less
sewing is required than when using a full-length Y.

The dorsal Y-cut is a popular approach, and can be made short or long, depending upon the size of the animal.

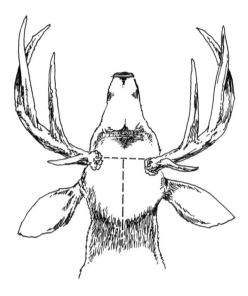

The T-cut calls for a direct incision across the skull from antler to antler, and then a dorsal cut over the neck to the shoulders.

Looking from the rear of the animal, imagine a short Y, with the top end of each leg of the Y connecting to the base of each horn or antler. Now imagine a T. This cut will go straight across from one antler to another, and then the incision running up the back of the neck will complete the T-shape with this initial incision. Next, a V-cut is simply a Y-cut that doesn't have a bottom leg. The 7-cut runs from the left antler or horn to the right, then from the right antler down the back, thus forming the shape of a 7. All of these cuts are useful, and which one you choose will ultimately be determined by what you like best. In the following chapters we will predominantly use the full-length or short Y, as these are probably used more than any other incision. In addition, these cuts are easier for beginners to use.

A full-length Y has been used for many years in taxidermy, and it offers the ease of test-fitting without having to remove

The V-cut is simply a variant on the Y-cut, and is an option for smaller animals that are easily skinned, or for delicate skins.

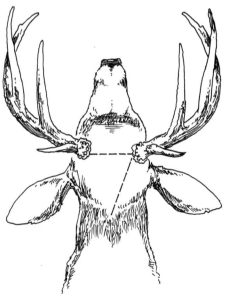

Depending upon the grain of the fur on a pelt, the 7-cut might be a more easily concealed cut because it runs at an angle.

the antlers or horns. Some taxidermists also say that this type of incision provides a flat skin which is somewhat easier to flesh and work with overall. The only real downside of a full-length Y is excessive sewing, which I abhor, and in very short-haired animals, the seam can be more difficult to conceal.

Life-Size Skinning

Dorsal Incision

Moving on to life-size skinning options, the most popular incision among taxidermists would probably be the *dorsal incision.* The dorsal cut is without a doubt the best for life-size critters, as it alleviates a bulk of sewing, and the incision along the backbone is more easily accessible than attempting to sew between the legs and in other tight places. (The only exception to this guideline would be a very thin-haired animal, such as a wild boar or some African animals. In these situations a *ventral incision* may be best—at least until the taxidermist has the ability to hide this type of incision with epoxy sculpt and paint.) As most big game is more thickly haired, I will refer to the dorsal incision in this book when dealing with life-size animals.

The dorsal incision calls for one straight cut only—from the base of the tail, along the backbone or slightly off to one side, up to the shoulder area on an animal such as a bear. An antlered or horned animal would require that the incision be continued up the back of the neck before making a V-cut just behind the antlers or horns, with the other options being a T-cut or a 7-cut. After this incision is complete, the skin will be peeled off, similar in fashion to a pair of coveralls that would zip up the back.

To begin the dorsal incision, roll the animal onto its chest and abdomen. If this isn't possible (as might be the case with a very large animal), you may have to allow the animal to lie on its side while you simply perform the skinning process at a different angle, turning the animal from side to side as the skinning process is completed. It is best to cut from the tail forward. Initially, insert the blade of a knife or scalpel at the base of the tail or slightly forward. Now, cut smoothly and as straight as possible toward the shoulder area. If a noticeable hair pattern exists along the center of the back, it might be best to slightly shift this cut to one side, to avoid disturbing this pattern. If no hair patterns exist, then simply follow the spine.

To create reference points for sewing after the initial incision is complete, make small corresponding cuts on each side of the incision. Make these cuts very small, almost unnoticeable, and spread them a couple of inches apart. Match these marks during the sewing process to ensure that the skin is sewn back to its original position.

At this point, depending on the animal, most skins can be easily peeled from the carcass with your hands. Using your fingers, grip one side at a time and begin pulling the skin free; you'll probably find the best start by pulling along the midsection. When the skin seems to have been pulled free as far as possible on one side, or if your initial incision didn't go far enough by a few inches, insert your hand between the skin and carcass and make the separation complete. Now, roll the animal onto its opposite side and repeat the pulling process.

Note: You will find that some animals are inherently easier to skin than others. The toughest are generally very large or have been allowed to cool thoroughly.

With the skin separated on both sides of the animal, begin working the skin free in the hip areas and down along the sides of each rear leg. Now you should have enough loose skin to pull it across the rear end of the animal, and to begin pulling the skin downward, toward the feet. But first you will have to either sever the tail from the carcass at its base, or pull the tail free of the skin by splitting the skin of the tail or just slipping it free. Don't misunderstand the term *slipping* here. Taxidermists use this word in two different ways. Here, the term means freeing the internal skeletal and muscle tissue from the tail skin without making an incision. But when referring to the preparation of a skin or while dealing with a skin, *slipping* (or *slippage,* as it is commonly called) indicates that bacteria has attacked the surface of a skin and caused the hair to slip from the skin surface. This type of slipping is not good. You'll learn not to confuse the two.

Ventral Incision

The *ventral incision* or *rug cut* is the next most popular cut for full-body preservations. This cut is made from the anal opening to the chest area. This incision should be only as deep as the outer skin layer. Cutting more deeply than this, along the frontal area of any game animal, will only serve to open the stomach area. And unless the animal being skinned has already been field dressed, opening the stomach area will only introduce body fluids to the hair or fur. Continue by cutting from each paw to the center of the body, where the initial incision in the center of the chest and stomach area will be intersected. To make these initial incisions properly, cut through the center of each paw, up to the knee or elbow area, and then gradually cut toward a perfect center of the inside of each leg. If you choose to use the rug cut, be very careful, making the cuts as straight as possible. Finish the skinning process as detailed in the dorsal incision description, above. The only true difference between the two is the location of the incision slated to pull the skin free of the carcass.

If you plan on a finished rug, then this method is the only option that you should consider. But if you want a life-size mount, a full rug cut is very time-consuming because it will necessitate more sewing in tight areas. On a positive note, the sewing attributed to a ventral incision is usually much easier to hide because it is on the underside of the mount.

Note: If you choose to continue your taxidermy career by eventually opening a taxidermy shop, you will find that most

The ventral incision is also called "the rug cut," for obvious reasons, but presents too much sewing for use in full-body mounts.

larger critters, no matter what the species, will come in already skinned using the ventral incision, or rug cut; then, the skin is removed from the carcass at the junction of the head and neck, as well as the ankles or wrists. Other items brought in to be mounted may be skinned completely, including the head and feet. Though it does happen, it is quite rare for a customer to show up at the door with a whole deer that hasn't been skinned, much less an elk or other large animal. But a person who hopes to become a competent taxidermist will need to know skinning methods for life-size mounts.

Skinning the Tail

How you choose to remove the tail section from the skin depends in large part on the particular animal and which preservation method you decide to use. The process of stripping the tail lends itself well to users of dry preservative. The dry preservative can be conveniently applied by carefully pushing the additive into the tail with a short length of wire. Doing it this way means there will be no seams to sew. Another option is to split the underside of the tail, applying dry preservative or tanning, depending on the chosen method, and then instead of sewing, you will use Super Glue to close the incision. This method is usually satisfactory, since the tails of most animals are thickly haired, and closing the seam in this manner should be nearly undetectable.

Deer tails can be slipped rather easily. This means that by holding the base of the tail at the point where it attaches to the body, and using a *tail-stripper*, the skin can be pulled free of the tail section, leaving a hollow area where the skeletal and muscular structure of the tail used to be. Tail-strippers are plier-shaped tools that have two differing sized holes in the working end that allow you to strip the skin from the muscle tissue and skeletal structure of a game animal. These are available at most taxidermy suppliers. If you don't have a tail-stripper, you can fashion one from either a pair of screwdrivers (coupled together), or by holding a pair of pliers loosely around the tail section, then pulling.

To slip the tail, simply wrap the stripper around the base of the tail and grip the tail at a point near the body; then, give a firm and even pull on the stripper, thus sliding the skin free of the tail bones. This may require some exertion, but the tail will eventually pop free.

Bear, antelope, and elk can be difficult if not impossible to slip, so the only alternative is to make an incision on the underside of the tail and skin it conventionally. Be very careful when skinning a tail, because the skin in this area can be very thin and it's easily ripped. If the skin is to be tanned, splitting and skinning the tail is the only option. This is also the only effective method to ensure proper salt penetration into the skin.

Once the tail section is free of the skin, continue by pulling the skin of the body toward the rear feet. Again, this is usually easily accomplished by using your hands. Should a tight place be encountered, use a knife or scalpel to continue freeing the skin. Be careful to avoid cutting any holes.

On most animals the skin will separate easily down to about the lower leg. Then, depending on the animal, you may need to make some *relief cuts*. Bears and mountain lions can usually be inverted all the way to the toes without these relief cuts. But for deer, antelope, and most other animals with hooves, these cuts will almost always have to be made. To make these relief cuts, start at the knee joint, on the back side of the leg, and make a straight cut to the hoof. Do this on all four legs and continue with the skinning process.

Hoofed Animals (Ungulates)

After your relief cuts are complete on an ungulate, continue freeing the skin on both rear legs toward the feet. If the animal being skinned has dew claws, be sure to cut them free to avoid ripping. Cutting the dew claws free during the skinning process is a simple matter of slowly working the knife or scalpel along the internal attachment point of the dew claw. The attachment point is similar to a joint, and only tissue connects each dew claw to bone and tendon. Sever this tissue and the dew claw will be free. After reaching the rear portion of the foot, the skinning process will slow somewhat, and the use of a short, curved knife will be required. Continue by pulling the skin, and slowly work a knife or scalpel around the foot until the top of the hooves are reached.

At this point, techniques can vary, and your choice of either dry preservative or tan will greatly influence what method you use here. Once the top of the hoof is reached, some taxidermists sever the hoof and lower leg joint, inject the area with a liquid preservative (a specially formulated preservative that can be used as a soak or an injectable preservative), then mount and allow to dry. These taxidermists insist that this method is fine. Others insist that the toes must be skinned in their entirety all the way to the last joint, which is nearly inside of the hoof. I have used both methods, and for general work, I have found that both are suitable. Also, keep in mind that if you plan to dry-preserve a skin, either method will be okay. But if you plan to tan the skin, the toes should be skinned completely to allow for proper saturation of the salt and other chemicals.

Skinning the toes on most any animal is rather tedious, and for many it can take longer to skin the four feet than it does to skin the rest of the animal. Once you reach the hoof area, slowly use the short, curved knife to cut alongside each joint. Be extra careful here not to cut yourself as you slowly sever the joining tissue, until you get a feel for where the last joint is located. I might not be explaining this in extreme detail, but keep in mind that even as a beginner, you will find your own way to do things, and learn to adapt to the requirements of each individual animal. Hooves and toes are just plain difficult. You have to slowly feel your way around them and cut as you go.

Bear and Mountain Lion Paws

The skinning of a paw is very different than skinning a hoof. For one thing, I believe they are not as difficult. Notice I didn't say they were *easier*, as the skinning of all feet is tedious and sometimes frustrating. There is nothing easy about it. As mentioned previously, the legs of most big game with paws can be inverted without making a relief cut on the rear of the leg. If, however, you find that inverting the skin is very difficult, you can make these same relief cuts on the back of each leg and simply sew the incisions during the mounting process.

At this point, be careful to avoid ripping the skin around the upper pads, which are only on the front legs. Continue skinning toward the foot area, and once the first toe joints are reached, attempt to get hold of the outermost toes; then, you can begin slowly inverting or pulling the toes free of the skin. As the outermost toes are the shortest, they are easiest to deal with before the longer middle toes are skinned. Slowly pull the toes free until a large percentage of the toe has been inverted; then, slowly work a short, curved knife alongside each toe bone until the last joint at the claw is severed. The best way I can describe this is to imagine that you're trying to skin a glove off the paw.

After the skin is separated from the rear feet, grasp the skin and pull it forward toward the chest and shoulder area. Once again, use a combination of pulling and carefully cutting to loosen the skin. Upon reaching the shoulder area, fold the front leg at the most flexible joint, closest to the shoulder (I refer to this as the *elbow*), and by pushing the front leg rearward, toward the back, pull the skin forward toward the head area. This will begin the skinning process of the front legs. Continue working your hands between the skin and carcass, forward of the shoulders. Once the skin is completely free around the elbow area, grip the elbow, and while pulling upward, begin pulling the skin down toward the feet. Note that the skin in the brisket area of many big-game animals can be very tender, so skin with caution. Use your knife slowly and deliberately in this sensitive area.

Skinning of the front paws is nearly identical to that of the back feet, with the only difference being the dew claws and pads located on the front legs. Slowly skin the leg and paw until the junction of the claw and last joint is found; then, sever and continue. After both front paws are completely skinned, the only areas where the skin will still be attached are the head and neck.

Skinning the Head and Neck Area for a Life-Size Mount

Continue by using a knife or scalpel, freeing the skin as you pull it toward the head. Skinning the neck area should pose no problems, but be extra careful not to make any cuts in the skin. Once the skull and neck junction is reached, you must skin the head. The exact method used depends on the specimen that you are working with. Although procedures are the same no matter what the animal, the difference lies in getting past the headgear on a deer, elk, or other antlered animal. For any animal without antlers, including bears, mountain lions, and most female animals, continue without making any further relief cuts. For antlered or horned animals, you must make a relief cut to the back of the head and neck—the Y-, T-, or V-cuts previously discussed on page 49—and then continue the skinning process as usual. While skinning the head, I recommend using the scalpel because it is much sharper than the knife and therefore can be used much more precisely. By gently pulling and making careful cuts, the head of most any animal should be skinned with relative ease. The reason the head is much more sensitive than other areas is obviously because it is the focus of attention on a mount. Therefore, any cuts or damaged areas will be more easily noticed. Also, in the head area there are various external and internal tissues that must remain attached to the skin. These tissues are for tucking and proper attachment to the manikin. In addition, leaving these tissues intact will ensure the integrity of the surrounding visible areas. These areas include the eyes, ears, nose, and mouth (or lips).

Ears

As you begin to pull the skin over the rear of the skull, you should start searching for the ear canal. While many taxidermists simply cut the ear free at the most convenient place, I prefer to cut deep within the ear canal to free the ear. This will ensure better anatomical correctness than an ear butt that has simply been stuffed with clay. To find the actual ear canal at the point where it enters the skull, begin by making several cuts into the muscle tissue, slightly to the side and near the rear of the skull. If the ear canal isn't found, simply move forward slightly and make another cut. As long as the cuts are being made into the muscle tissue alone, no harm is being done. Once each ear canal is found and severed, continue by slowly peeling the skin forward.

Eyes, Mouth, and Nose

Slow down your skinning as you get closer to the eyes, and take a moment to assess how you're going to work around them. If possible, insert a finger between the eyelid and the eyeball, and then pull the skin away from the skull. This will help eliminate the possibility of cutting the inner eyelid. With the skin pulled away from the skull, continue skinning slowly. As you near the rear corner of the eye, make sure to make your cuts very close to the skull. Once the rear corner of the eye is cut, the remainder of the eye can be cut free from the skull without damage to the eyelid.

In bears, mountain lions, caribou, and antelope, the tear ducts are either nonexistent or very small. But for whitetail, and especially mule deer and elk, the tear ducts are much larger and can easily be cut if you're not extremely careful. To skin past the tear ducts, use the knife to skin slowly at the front corner of the eye socket, and then as the orifice is located, use the knife to cut deeply around the tear duct, carefully detaching it. Try to remove the tear duct without making any holes in it; if a minor cut does occur, however, it can be repaired without too much difficulty. For elk and mule deer, cuts in the tear ducts are nearly impossible to avoid.

After you pull the skin forward of both eyes and the tear duct area, concentrate on the rear corners of the mouth. Cutting the mouth free with plenty of lip skin will ensure that you will be able to properly tuck the skin on a closed-mouth mount.

Doing so will also allow for plenty of skin that can be tucked into a manikin or along a jawset on an open-mouth mount.

Begin cutting the lips free by first feeling with your finger for the rear teeth, on the exterior of the skin. Once you feel these teeth, make a small but penetrating cut slightly behind them. Then, as an opening is made, insert one finger and pull the lip line away from the skull. As you skin forward, leaving plenty of lip line, you must slow down to correctly cut the skin free of the front of the mouth and to separate the nose area properly.

To cut the nose free, make an initial cut (depending on the size of the animal) at least an inch behind the front of the nose or as soon as cartilage is encountered. This area should consist of cartilage and should be easy to cut. On smaller animals you may have to move slightly toward the tip of the nose in order to avoid cutting into bone. With the nose and front lip line severed, the skin should be completely free of the carcass. Now you are ready to begin the fleshing and the chosen preservation process.

Guidelines for Optimum Skinning Results

1. Leave as much flesh on the carcass as possible.

This will help to reduce the length of the fleshing process. To accomplish this, use your hands to pull the skin away from the carcass as much as possible during the skinning process. This is where the skin should normally separate from any muscle tissue. Cutting, although a must in some areas, can leave large amounts of muscle tissue attached to the skin if you aren't careful.

2. Avoid making excessive cuts.

This only leads to extra sewing, which takes time and can reduce the quality of the finished product. Extra cuts do occasionally happen, even in the hands of careful, experienced taxidermists, but as experience builds, you will find yourself reducing these unnecessary cuts to a minimum. Decreasing the amount of these cuts comes from learning the color changes that are evident along the skin, muscle, and tissue lines that vary from one animal to another, and the different body areas for each animal.

3. Take your time, but don't waste time.

Although this may sound contradictory, it actually rings true. You must move at a proper pace while skinning, as this helps to avoid any excessive damage to the skin. On the other hand, completing the skinning in as little time as possible can prevent any slippage that may otherwise occur. As with everything, practice will improve your skill level; the amount of time you will require for the skinning process will decrease as you gain in experience.

4. Make your incisions as straight as possible.

Maintaining straight incisions and occasionally marking corresponding skin sides with a very small cut or hole can be extremely helpful during the sewing process. This will allow both sides of the skin to match up properly, allowing any hair patterns to flow out evenly. Matching skin sides will also alleviate any binding that may occur should the skin be shifted from its original position.

5. Choose the skinning method according to the mount desired.

If I have any say-so, I will always use a dorsal incision for a life-size mount and a V-cut for a shoulder mount. This is for several reasons. Obviously, less sewing is needed, the incisions are much easier to reach, and the seams are easier to pull tight; you won't have to sew between the legs and along the legs in spaces that can sometimes be pretty tight. But sometimes you have to let the mount itself dictate the proper incision. Read the skin carefully and be willing to be flexible when necessary.

If you plan for a rug, then a rug cut is the only reasonable option. For a full-body mount positioned on its belly, a short ventral incision is best. Are you making such a mount for a competition? Are you very picky and precise? If you say yes to either of these questions, then you'll want to hide the seam as much as possible, and a ventral cut is the only way to go. But for commercial mounts, when no judge will be critiquing the mount, a dorsal incision will probably work just fine, even for that full-body mount on its stomach.

CHAPTER 5

Fleshing the Pelt

After the skinning process is complete, your attention will be turned toward properly fleshing the skin, which includes the removal of all muscle tissue, thinning the skin slightly, and splitting or turning of the face. Initially, small projects such as shoulder-mount deer or antelope can be completed with a knife, scissors, and plenty of patience. Turning and splitting of the face is best accomplished by hand, using a scalpel or a very sharp knife. However, fleshing from the neck rearwards toward the shoulders or the rest of the body is best completed using a fleshing machine, which I highly recommend.

As with any new piece of equipment, it will take some time to get used to a fleshing machine. My first experience with a flesher was while fleshing a deer cape. When I finished, hair was sticking through the inside of the skin and holes were plentiful—definitely not a professional job, and actually, the skin was beyond repair. But a good lesson was learned from that first attempt, and now my skins are top-notch. Always practice on skin scraps or on animal skins that are disposable, not on an actual job, because you *will* make mistakes while you're learning. A good practice medium is the back hide of a deer, because they are easy to obtain and provide a large working area. In my experience, antelope skins are extremely thin and difficult to work with, while other larger critters such as elk, moose, or bears are often too difficult or too costly to obtain just for practice. But if a top-quality, finished product isn't the goal, then by all means, practice with whatever is available. You will quickly learn that each skin has individual characteristics, while other traits are shared.

FLESHING MACHINES

You will find that fleshing machines vary in quality as well as price. Some of the best commercial machines on the market may not be ideal for beginners, but once you have had some experience with a high-end machine, they will be a pleasure to work with, more so than a low-end version. Most high-end commercial machines have slightly stronger motors which turn blades at higher rpms than some of the cheaper machines. This enables the user to produce a large amount of work in a short amount of time. But before the user is proficient at using a rotary knife, these high-end machines can make a terrible mess because they remove flesh and excess skin so quickly.

A fleshing machine is also known as a "rotary knife" because the most common type incorporates a round metal disc that has been sharpened along the edge. The outermost portion, about one-quarter inch, is angled to about 75 degrees. The disk itself is attached directly to a bearing, which is connected by a pulley to an electric motor that rapidly turns the blade, thus creating a spinning knife edge. All proper rotary blades come with blade guards attached to each side, and you will learn how to work with them in place. Don't remove them. Doing so would put you at risk for serious cuts to the hand and forearm.

ALTERNATIVES TO THE FLESHING MACHINE

For many years before the introduction of electric fleshers, most taxidermists completed the fleshing process by hand. Today, the majority use a machine, but I do know professional taxidermists who still choose to hand-flesh exclusively. As a beginner, you'll be wise to learn the basics of hand-fleshing, as it is an important element in our bag of tricks, and can be beneficial for future reference. For example, some taxidermists strictly hand-flesh prior to the tanning stage; then, they will use the machine only during the shaving process, which is done after the initial pickling. No set rule applies here. You may find that hand-fleshing is sufficient for all of your projects. And if you decide to use only dry preservative, or to send your skins to a commercial tannery, this will also significantly reduce your need for a machine.

A primary attribute of hand-fleshing is the minimal start-up cost. The price of a commercially manufactured fleshing beam, which is used to position a small portion of a skin onto the working area for hand-fleshing, is usually less than $50. Or you can simply make your own out of PVC pipe and wooden slats, to create a rounded beam; thus providing a working area that can be used to lay skins and hair down, and flesh can be removed properly from the skin side.

The cost-conscious taxidermist can make a fleshing beam out of PVC pipe.

Building a Tabletop Fleshing Beam

Building your own tabletop fleshing beam requires approximately a dozen 1½- to 2-inch wood screws, a 3-foot section of 4- to 6-inch diameter PVC pipe, and some wooden strips of varying size. Begin by cutting one end of the pipe at a 60-degree pitch so that when it is attached to the table, the pipe juts out at 45 degrees or less in relation to the flat surface. If you feel this angle is suitable for laying skins and fleshing, continue. If not, adjust the angle of the cut slightly until a preferred beam angle is achieved. While some may like a steep angle for their beam, others may prefer an angle that is nearly flat. Because these materials are inexpensive, you can always adjust the angle once you determine what best suits your needs.

Once the pipe is angled correctly and attached, secure wooden bracing to one end, on each side. I use 2X2s, but whatever is available and works best for you should do the trick. The length can vary as all beams are built to suit a specific user. A good average length for these bracing strips would be eighteen inches, but you can adjust according to your preference.

Once the wooden legs are attached to each side of the pipe, drill a hole into the center of the angled end, which will serve to secure the fleshing beam to the worktable (see photo on previous page). Insert a wood screw through the predrilled hole and tighten to the table. This will prevent the beam from sliding around as fleshing takes place. Now the fleshing beam is complete and ready to use.

Next, you must purchase a knife or tool designed for fleshing. Any basic knife with a blade that is twelve inches or longer is sufficient. Something similar to a butcher knife is ideal, and most can be had for about $15. However, you can use a *T-handle fleshing knife*, which is designed specifically for hand-fleshing.

Although it costs more than a butcher knife—about $60—it is much easier to use and generally produces better results. Once you have a fleshing knife and have assembled or purchased a fleshing beam, you will have all the tools required to properly flesh most deer-sized animals.

In addition to both a rotary knife and a fleshing beam, you will need a small wooden beam that comes to a small blunt point. This beam will be used primarily to hand-flesh small facial areas, legs, and most any tight spot on the skin. To make this *small fleshing beam*, cut a 1X2 strip of wood, about 12 to 14 inches in length. Angle the working end slightly to come to a blunt point, small enough to stick into the eye hole of a deer or bear. Sand thoroughly to ensure that there are no sharp edges, splinters, or knots on the beam. Then use a wood screw to attach the square end to a workbench. Some taxidermists cut the handle off a wooden baseball bat, sharpen it, and then secure this customized section to a workbench.

A small fleshing beam, which you can easily make yourself, is necessary for the detail work on facial areas and paws.

A particular advantage of hand-fleshing during the learning stage is the ability to have more control over how much flesh is actually being removed. The only disadvantage to hand-fleshing is that it requires much more time and yields results which are inferior to those of an experienced machine user.

Turning of the Face

I generally turn the ears and split the eyes, ears, and nose prior to the regular fleshing process, although this isn't mandatory. I like this method because once the face is turned, I can concentrate fully on fleshing instead of having to stop to deal with the head. This can be reversed, however, as some people prefer to do the bulk of the fleshing of the body and facial areas using a machine before they begin the final turning and hand-fleshing of the face. As mentioned before, you will soon adopt your own methods based on personal preference.

Turning of the face is the expression used for separating or splitting the skin and tissues that surround the eyes, lips, and nose. To better understand the term *turning*, imagine folding a piece of cardboard in half and using an adhesive to glue it shut. What you have is a continuous piece of cardboard, but to get the cardboard—or, in our situation, the skin—in a form where it can be properly preserved and worked with, it must lay flat. To do this, you must cut through the bonded area. This will provide a continuation of skin in the eye, nose, and lip area that can be thinned, trimmed, and then tucked properly during later stages of the mounting process.

In addition, the ears will be "turned" inside out, ready for the insertion of an ear liner, or to be filled with Bondo, which is used to provide a rigid and desired shape for the ear. If you were to leave the ear unturned before continuing with the mounting process, the ear would eventually shrivel and curl, leading to a very non-lifelike result. (As you progress and learn more about taxidermy, you may see preservation materials that suggest the taxidermist can simply inject the ears with this or that particular solution and then complete the mounting process without turning the ears. Though this will work fine for numerous small-game animals, many taxidermists have found the end product of this nonturning approach to be less than desirable on big-game animals.)

Turning and splitting the face is a delicate process, and because of the very thin tissues in this key area, you must proceed with caution. I prefer a scalpel for this work, as few knives can be sharpened well enough to cut without having to be pushed slightly. On the other hand, a scalpel may prove to be *too* sharp for a beginner, and could easily cut through the tender skin, causing even more problems. It is important to proceed carefully with whatever method you choose.

The Lips

I usually start the splitting process at the lips and nose and then work back. Hold the lip between your thumb and fingers and slowly begin to split it. Do this by cutting very slowly between the skin and the tissue that is basically doubled back onto it. The scalpel will separate the tissues so the lips can lie perfectly flat.

Continue around the lip line until each lip is completely separated. You will quickly acquire a feel for what is correct. The skin will feel flat and uniform, not lumpy, because lumpiness occurs when an area isn't split all the way to the edge. With the lip line complete, I begin to work with the nose.

The Nose

While all facial areas are important, the nose is one of the more prominent features and is a real eye-catcher. When looking at a mount, one of the first things we notice is the eyes, probably followed closely by the nose. I have seen mounts that were put together well with the exception of the nose, and this flaw basically ruined the entire mount. If you look closely at some poor mounts, the nose may seem to have large waves or bumps. This is due to improper turning or fleshing of the nose. Remember—the more flesh that is left attached to the skin, the bigger the chance that shrinkage can occur. So it is very important to split the nose thoroughly and flesh it as thinly as possible.

To begin, lay the nose, with its inner layer facing you, on the ends of the index and middle fingers and use the thumb to manipulate the flesh. Now use the scalpel to cut through the center of the nose between each nostril. The nose is made up of cartilage, but this shouldn't pose a problem. Cut slowly to prevent slicing the outside of the nose pad. You will quickly learn to feel with your fingers to determine thickness and how close you are cutting to the surface of the skin. Make the cut as close to the center of the nose as possible. With the center cut, begin to separate the surrounding cartilage from the skin itself. If this is done slowly, you shouldn't have any trouble. But one place that may be more difficult than the rest is what's known as the *wing area* of the nose. Because of the way these outer-edged flaps of the nose are shaped, this area is usually the toughest to thoroughly split. Work slowly and carefully through these areas, checking often to see how much more needs to be split.

The Eyes

With the nose complete, you can turn your attention to the eyes. Peel the skin up the snout, just up to the eye socket. Place the index finger through the eye opening and begin separating the membrane along the eyelid. Use the scalpel to separate the lid across its entire circumference, opening the flesh all the way to the section containing a fatty membrane. This membrane runs along the very edge of the tissue that normally surrounds the eye itself. This fatty tissue helps to anchor the eyelashes, and it provides a soft wiping action as the eye is opened and closed. If this fatty tissue is not removed, more shrinkage than normal will take place. After splitting both eyelids, continue to the ears.

The Ears

To turn the ears properly, begin by separating the muscle tissue at the ear base from the surrounding skin. Then slowly use your fingers and a scalpel to separate the skin just beyond the base of the ear. For most big game, continue by utilizing an ear opener, as discussed in the tools section in chapter 2. Slowly insert the ear opener and begin to gently work the ear open until the edges are nearly reached—but not entirely. Should you attempt to open the ears all the way to the edges using the openers, you will more than likely split the ear open. So when the ear is turned within an approximate half-inch of the edge, invert the ear and continue to carefully turn the ear entirely to the edge using only your fingers. It's important to try to do this without separating the skin of the ear at the edges.

Ear Problems That May Be Encountered

During your initial attempts, it might be best to avoid turning the ears entirely to the edge. Doing so will avoid the possibility of making large holes in the ear that can be difficult for the beginner to repair. Also note that in some animals, the ears can be difficult to turn using an ear opener. These animals may have severe damage to the ear from fighting, ticks, or a variety of other reasons. If you encounter an ear that is very difficult to open using ear openers, simply work slowly with your hands and a scalpel until the edges are reached. Because they stick up, badly mounted ears will call attention to their unsightliness as much as a poorly mounted nose does.

Once the entire face is split and turned, attention will shift to the fleshing of the cape or the remainder of the body, legs, and facial areas for a life-size skin. Whatever method is chosen (rotary knife or by hand), I have always preferred to flesh from the tail forward. For bear and a few other animals, this is much better, so I have simply gotten into the habit of doing all skins this way.

FLESHING WITH A ROTARY KNIFE

Fleshing with a rotary knife is a time-effective method, and once you've become familiar with using one, you will soon be able to thin and flesh the thinnest to the thickest of skins in short order. Just go slowly until you are thoroughly familiar with the particular model being used. If you buy a brand-new machine, it may come with a video that demonstrates and fully explains the proper fleshing methods. If not, you could purchase a quality fleshing instruction video separately.

To begin fleshing, grip a portion of the skin in your right hand, as most fleshing machines work from left to right, and then hold an adjacent, forward portion of skin in your left hand. The width at which you place your hands can vary slightly. While you're learning, spread your hands apart only about eight to ten inches. Initially, a narrow grip will allow you to work slowly and on a small section at a time. By doing so, if you happen to cut the skin, the cut should be relatively small. As you gain experience you will be able to gradually widen your grip.

Continue by slowly pulling the skin from left to right, and you will quickly see any attached muscle tissue begin to peel off. For animals such as antelope and bear, the skin is mostly thin, so you will want to just skim the surface and remove only muscle tissue and fat without thinning the skin. Do this by ad-

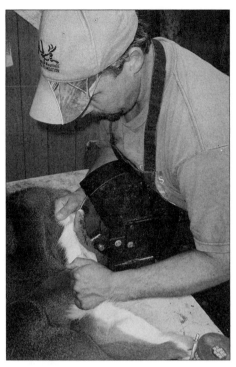

In the beginning, go slowly with a rotary knife and flesh small sections at a time. With experience, you'll gain speed and accuracy.

justing the guards and the angle of the blade to a very shallow bite (instructions for doing this should accompany every model). Tracks made by the rotary knife are very easy to see, so once an area is free of flesh, begin work on a new area. Do this until the entire cape or body area up to the neck is clean and free of any fleshy tissue.

Fleshing the Legs and Face

Though the leg areas from just above the knee to the foot or hoof of most big-game animals require very little or no fleshing, you will be wise to make certain these areas are thoroughly cleaned and ready for preservation. Do this by sliding these lower leg sections up onto the small wooden fleshing beam, pulling them like a shirtsleeve onto an arm. Then begin to slowly and lightly cut away any remaining flesh; very little if any flesh should exist in these areas. To begin with, I would recommend a knife, as sometimes a scalpel can be too sharp for these thin areas. If only a small amount of muscle tissue is attached to the leg area, you may choose to skip the fleshing procedure. Also, if using dry preservative, you can use your hands to pull free any small amounts of tissue once the preservative is applied.

The last area I flesh is usually the face. The face is probably the most delicate area that you will work with, and though experienced users of a fleshing machine can work in these tight, sensitive areas, I generally elect to use a scalpel when completing the fleshing procedures. As mistakes are tougher to fix and the skin is generally thinner in the facial area, proceed with extra caution, no matter what method is chosen.

Hand-Beaming Very Thin Areas

Begin by sliding the head onto the small wooden fleshing beam, and then position the portion of the upper lip adjacent to the nose pad onto the end of the beam nearest you. Then, as you thoroughly flesh each small section of lip line, rotate the cape until the entire lip line is complete. For fleshing these thin areas I have gotten used to (and am fully comfortable with) using a scalpel, but a beginner may want to use a *skife knife*, which is a razor blade with a guard attached. These can be purchased directly from taxidermy suppliers. Another option is your regular knife. As stated before, I can't get a knife sharp enough to suit my needs, so for that reason I would recommend a skife knife.

Now, slowly begin to flesh the lip area until only very thin skin remains. On many areas a properly fleshed skin will allow light to fully penetrate the skin. Rotate the lip line slightly, and then repeat. Do this until the entire length of the lip line is properly fleshed. Now move on to the nose.

Insert the end of the beam into each nostril. Make certain that the fleshing beam being used is free of any lumps. A smooth surface is important because if a lump exists, it can easily cause you to cut a hole into the skin during the fleshing process. Once the beam is in place within one nostril, slowly shave the surrounding area until it is thin and free of flesh. This can be tricky, as the attached cartilage should be completely removed. It is very easy to cut completely through the skin's surface if you aren't extremely careful. Continue by fleshing the opposite nostril, making certain that all excess flesh and cartilage in the nose-pad area is thoroughly removed.

After the nose is complete, pull the entire facial skin onto the beam until the eyelid surrounds the point of the beam. All facial areas are very thin and can be damaged easily, but the eye area may be the most vulnerable, so use extreme care at this stage.

With the skin in place on the beam, flesh slowly toward the eye opening. In the eyebrow areas of most animals, the flesh is a bit thicker than in the rest of the face, so make certain that it is removed. Now, you should have previously turned the eye in such a way that you can easily see a row of fat along the very edge of the eyelid. To complete the thorough fleshing of the eye, this fat must be removed. After some practice this becomes much easier, but the skin in this area is only a fraction of a millimeter thick, similar to the thickness of paper, so go slowly.

Once both eyelids are properly fleshed, begin to slowly rotate the face using the eye as a center point locked onto the beam. As you are rotating the face, carefully cut free any remaining flesh. The flesh between the eye and nose, eye and opposite eye, and eye and rear jaw all needs to be removed. Then, place the lower jaw onto the beam and remove any excess flesh there. For the whisker area, I usually thin some, but not too much, because if you cut too much flesh from this area, the whiskers may fall out. Finally, use a small pair of scissors to snip free any small amounts of remaining flesh anywhere on the skin.

At this point the fleshing process should be complete, and the skin ready to either dry-preserve and mount, or salt and prepare for the tanning process. If using the dry-preservative method, I would suggest getting the skin as free of flesh as possible. If tanning is chosen, small amounts of flesh can be left for now. Later during the tanning process, this excess will be removed. (When skin is prepped for tanning, any excess flesh will be thinned during the pickling stage, as the pickle fully saturates the skin.)

Note: If you do choose to shave after pickling, the procedures are identical to the ones taken thus far. Drain the skin, and then continue with the previously described procedures, removing any remaining skin. Remember—the primary goal of shaving after the pickle is to thin the skin, so be very careful as removing too much may weaken the skin.

BEAM-FLESHING

Fleshing using only a knife or fleshing tool and a beam is effective, although a machine will generally do a quicker and more thorough job.

To use the beam designed for hand-fleshing, lay the skin onto the larger beam affixed to the top of your workbench, with the rear of the cape or life-size skin closest to you. Lightly lean into the rear of the beam, as this should help to hold the skin in place. Then, using a knife or fleshing tool, slowly cut any flesh free from the skin as you push down toward the table. As an area is cleaned, rotate the skin slightly until all skin in this area has been removed.

Once you've completed this area, continue with the methods described in the "Fleshing the Legs and Face" section (see pages 75 and 76). While using a fleshing beam, make certain that the skin lays flat and that no lumps exist between the skin and the beam. These lumps (caused by cockleburs, mud clods, or other contaminants that may exist in the animal's hair) can increase the risk of punctures in the skin.

With a well-fleshed and prepared skin, you are on your way to a top-quality mount. A lot of the "grunt work" is now behind you.

CHAPTER 6

Preserving the Skin

After the skinning process is complete, you must determine which preservation method to use. Preserving the skin allows you to enjoy your work of art for as long as possible, hopefully a lifetime. Your first mount is no exception. Even as your skills progress—and I can assure you that they will if you devote time to the art—you will enjoy looking back on your first few attempts. Not only at the trophy you collected, but also the improvements you have made along the way. Because you will want this creation to last, you must choose and properly utilize the best preservation methods that are available. Ultimately, only you can make this decision.

Which do you choose—dry preserve or tan? This is a common question among beginners. And there is no clear-cut answer for all applications. If you speak to anyone in the taxidermy industry, you will be pulled into the controversy of preservation methods. Debate has raged for years about dry preservative versus a true tan. Most likely, the debate will continue for decades to come unless some new, as-yet-unknown chemical arrives that makes both dry preservation and tanning obsolete.

As for myself, I fully believe that both are viable options, and your choice depends primarily on the animal being preserved. For example, I would never tan a squirrel because I feel there is no need to do so. However, there are those who would, in fact, insist upon tanning a squirrel. On the other hand, I would never, and I repeat, *never,* dry-preserve a moose as the skin thickness may inhibit proper saturation, or a bear as the skins tend to be tremendously greasy and will only cause problems long after the mount is completed, but there are some who insist that dry preservative will work on any animal.

In my taxidermy shop, I use both dry preservative and an in-house tan—and, of course, I use a commercial tannery for larger projects or when time is short. The decision about which preservation method to use depends on the particular project, the type and size of the animal, and any potential time constraints. In short, I believe both methods have their place.

Most advocates of dry preservative say it is quick and reliable, and they believe that a great product can be achieved when using it. Many respected taxidermists throughout the country use this method exclusively, and consistently put out quality work—work that is better, in fact, than the product of some others who may abide by a strict "tan everything" rule. Yet a friend of mine who competes often in world competitions consistently earns ribbons, and has done so with both dry-preserved and tanned skins.

The dry-preservative approach consists of a thorough fleshing and washing, and then an application of a dry preservative. This makes for pretty quick work, as the taxidermist can skin, flesh, wash, preserve, and mount, all in a day or two. Dry preservatives vary in quality, however, and not all are created equal. Most companies offer dry preservatives intended for use in a specific preservative recipe.

Then there are those taxidermists who swear by a tanned product only. They insist tanning is the sole method for competition as well as commercial work. All tanning advocates argue that tanning is a much more effective method of preservation, with greater ease of use resulting in longer product life. Frankly, most dedicated competition participants use only tanned skins in their work, although as my friend proves, there are exceptions.

Complete tanning involves a full list of steps that traditionally includes salting, pickling, and a final tanning soak or brush-on tan. There are also more modern methods that involve a simple soaking in a tanning solution, although some die-hard tanning advocates say this is not a true tan, and is actually no better than using a dry preservative. Within the tanning realm there

Before you start tanning, you need to have a totally dry, clean, even fluffy pelt, and a tumbler can be a big help in creating a really good mount.

are an abundance of tans to choose from, and we will discuss them in more detail later in the chapter.

As with other decisions you make in the taxidermy field, the preservation method you choose is strictly a personal decision. But the more you know about a variety of methods, the more informed your decision will be. As a beginner, you will be able to perform preservation work with most animals. When it comes to bear products, however (whether it's a shoulder mount, life-size, or rug), newcomers should send this work to a competent commercial tannery. Do not attempt to tan or dry-preserve these skins. Bears are very greasy, and therefore difficult to work with. Some taxidermists preserve bears themselves, but I choose to let those with commercial-grade degreasers and other equipment take care of this tough chore, and in return, I am provided with a product that is much more pleasurable to work with.

DRY PRESERVATIVE

Dry preservative is a powdered chemical substance that if applied properly will preserve and protect the skin from bacterial growth. Most dry preservatives are a mix of chemicals that include ingredients designed to discourage bugs from infesting the specimen, as well as those which may help eliminate odors. Moths and other flesh-eating insects can be detrimental to a mount, so a bug deterrent is one of the real advantages of a dry preservative. (While most people agree that this bug-proofing will eventually dissipate, leaving the trophy vulnerable to infestation, I haven't found this to be the case. Neither I nor many of the longtime taxidermists I know who regularly use dry preservative have had any problems with bugs.)

On the downside, if you don't use a preservative with a deterrent, you will eventually see bug problems. To avoid this possibility, the taxidermist or owner of a mount must monitor and treat all mounts with a bug deterrent at least every four to six months. Though some people may call any powdered method a "quick tan," there is actually no stabilization of the structural proteins within the skin when using dry preservative. So while dry preservative is a viable option in some situations, it should never be considered a true tan.

A dry-preserved skin is essentially rawhide that has had the moisture removed. It can return to a raw state at any time, should enough moisture contaminate the skin. But the moisture content in the air would have to be extremely high for a very long period of time in order to return a properly dry-preserved skin to a raw state. Note that the same moisture-laden air would not return a tanned skin to rawhide, but would have a harmful effect on skins that have been properly tanned.

Because skin is made up of approximately 60 to 70 percent fluid, it could easily be damaged by bacteria if left in its rawhide state. Remember that during field-care procedures, moisture and warmth can combine to promote bacteria growth. To help eliminate moisture in the skin, dry preservative is composed heavily of *desiccants*. Desiccants are chemical drying agents that absorb and help prevent the recurrence of moisture in the skin. This is partly how the name "dry preservative" came about, since it preserves by using a drying action. And because bacteria, which break down the epidermis of the skin, can't exist in a moisture-free environment, no deterioration takes place. Therefore, the desiccant-laden dry preservative effectively preserves the skin by pulling moisture from it and keeping it dry.

A second major ingredient of a dry preservative is a *surfactant*. Surfactants help the desiccant penetrate the skin and be absorbed, allowing the desiccant to do its job. The surfactant lowers the surface tension of the moisture in the skin, countering the natural characteristic of raw skin to repel foreign substances, and thus allowing the skin to absorb the preservative.

There are some helpful things you can do to alleviate any problems associated with the dry-preservative method. First, you can allow whatever dry preservative you choose to penetrate the skin thoroughly. To help this process along, apply a generous amount of the preservative and then fold up the skin and lay it on a towel in a refrigerated or cool area. Let it stay there for a short time, approximately 30 minutes, but no more than a couple hours, while preparing the manikin for completion, and then remove the skin and shake any excess preservative free. If you applied the substance properly, the skin will have absorbed plenty of the preservative.

Another issue associated with dry preservative is the fact that significant shrinkage can occur. To alleviate this problem, I recommend that a high-quality "hide paste" or epoxy adhesive be used in crucial areas. Epoxy adhesive is a step above the regular hide paste, and I find that it will lock down the skin before it has time to dry, shrink, and pull itself away from its intended position. Epoxy adhesives will also promote minimal shrinkage as compared to a generic hide paste.

I feel that a disregard for dry preservative as a viable preservation option stems from taxidermists who in the past have not given this method a fair shake. The taxidermist who had trouble with dry preservative probably didn't flesh the skin properly or take accurate measurements of the animal being mounted. These two sources of trouble are probably the most common among dry-preservative users. What a dry-preservative user must understand is that any flesh or thick-skinned areas will shrink considerably more than a well-fleshed, thin-skinned area. Also, a raw skin can be stretched considerably more than a tanned one. While both a tanned or dry-preserved skin will shrink at some point, the greatest amount of shrinking of a tanned skin takes place during the tanning process, whereas all shrinkage that will occur in a dry-preserved skin does so *after* mounting. Therefore, when using dry preservative, you must get exact measurements of the carcass and be careful to flesh the skin thoroughly. Following these guidelines should produce satisfactory results that last a lifetime.

Note: Once a mount is complete, keep it in a controlled environment. Ideal conditions are between 60 and 80 degrees Fahrenheit, with low humidity. The same goes for drying and storing tanned products.

TANNING

Understanding the chemical composition changes that take place within a skin during the tanning process may help you decide which method to use. Taxidermists who choose the tanning method usually do so because they like the fact that the skin is more stable during the mounting process (less shrinkage) than with dry preservative. Many also believe that using a complete tan offers a softer, more realistic appearance to the skin after drying and finishing.

To understand this stability, you must first know what animal skin actually comprises. (We aren't scientists here, so I will attempt to make this as simple as possible.) Skin is a complex mixture of moisture (mostly water) and proteins. Within this wide range of proteins there are those which are soluble and those which are insoluble. I once read a very accurate description of skin composition in a taxidermy manual published by *Breakthrough* magazine. The manual said that we should think of a skin as a leafy tree. The trunk and limbs can be considered the structural or insoluble proteins. The leaves represent the blood, fats, and soluble proteins. To stabilize a skin, you must first remove these leaves, leaving only the leafless limbs. But you can't stop at this stage, or your tree limbs will eventually collapse for lack of anything that supports them or provides them with nutrients.

Translated into taxidermy terms, this means that when dry preservative is used, much of the soluble proteins are pulled from the skin, with nothing to replace them. This is why a bit more shrinkage occurs in a dry-preserved skin, in addition to the skin being more brittle after fully drying. However, when true tanning is completed properly, the soluble proteins—the leaves of the tree—are replaced with *tannins*. Tannins can be thought of as artificial leaves, which act as a sort of filler that attaches to the insoluble structure. These tannins will also help lubricate the structure, preventing it from eventually collapsing and becoming glued together. Thus, tanning produces less shrinkage and a more pliable, more stable product.

In recent years new methods have been developed that shortcut the full process. But still, if a step is dismissed, some important part of the tanning process is eliminated. Because of this, die-hard tanning advocates insist that these new procedures and chemicals are no better than dry preservative, and they stick to the old tried-and-true methods they have become so familiar with.

Six Steps of the Tanning Process

If you choose to conventionally tan a skin (which I feel should be mandatory for everyone who attempts taxidermy), you will follow six distinct steps:

Step 1: The Salting Process

Once the skin has been properly fleshed and the eyes, lips, nose, and ears turned, you will begin by applying a medium layer of salt. This will extract the soluble proteins—blood, fats, and some of the oils—from the skin. Once the salt is applied and rubbed into every area of the skin, roll or fold up the skin with all cuts and openings to one side so adequate drainage can take place. Then, set aside this rolled-up skin, preferably on a gentle slope with the openings on the low side. Placing the skin on an upside-down milk crate also works well. This will allow the fluids to drain properly from the skin.

After twenty-four hours, unroll the skin and shake free any excess salt. Repeat the salting procedure. Once the second salting has taken place, you may continue the tanning process, or store the skin in a dry environment until you are ready to continue.

Note: If you live in an area with high humidity and you choose to store the skin until a later time, it may be wise to place it in the freezer. When sending the skin to a tannery, I like to open it and hang it in a breezy area or in front of a fan. This helps to further dry the skin, prohibiting any drainage that may occur during shipping.

Step 2: The Salt Solution

After completing the salting process, you will be ready to proceed. First, shake the excess salt from the skin. Continue by placing the skin into a salt solution with a ratio of 1½ cups of salt to 1 gallon of cold water. The amount of solution depends on the size and number of skins to be soaked. (For example, for one deer cape, I start with about two gallons of solution.) Soak the skin for approximately thirty minutes. This salt solution is important, as it prevents the skin from suffering what is called "acid swelling" in the pickle solution (the very next step), and it will also alleviate or slow any bacterial growth.

This soak is also important for a *flinted* skin (a skin that is sun-dried raw, with no salt) or thoroughly dried skins, as it will prep the skin and allow the pickle to penetrate much more quickly. If you are dealing with a flint-dried skin, allow the skin to sit in this salt solution for several hours before placing it directly into the pickle solution. Though the rehydrating process may take a bit longer when using the pickle solution, rehydration will help prevent the growth of any undue bacteria that may otherwise attack the skin.

Step 3: The Pickle Bath

Now, place the pliable skin into a pickle bath, which is a mixture of salt and acid. A pickle bath is used to further dissolve and remove the soluble proteins within the skin. The acid in the pickle bath will also break up the natural bonds of the proteins and prepare the skin fibers to bond with the tannins that will be introduced in the tanning bath. Taxidermy suppliers offer several different kinds of acid for pickle baths. Once again, most taxidermists who tan skins themselves have a favorite acid. To get started, I would recommend Safetee Acid; later, you can experiment with other acids. (I use oxalic acid, but more stringent safety measures must be taken when using this or many of the other types of acid that are available to the taxidermist.) Safetee Acid is a new formula that has proven to be less harmful to the user and the environment than many of the other acids available. It will also maintain a low, steady pH level, which is preferable.

In a pickle bath you must maintain a pH level between 1.5 and 2.5 for mammal skins, with 2.0 being ideal. Most acid comes with instructions on how to achieve the proper pH levels. Soak time varies with the thickness of the skin as well as the pickle of choice. A safe rule for a deer or antelope cape is to soak the skin in the pickle for twenty-four hours; remove; flesh it again; and then redeposit it in the bath for an additional twenty-four hours. At this point the skin should be ready to place into the tan. For elk, moose, and other large mammals, these soaking periods should be increased to forty-eight hours or more before the fleshing and thinning, as well as after.

If timing prohibits the prompt removal of a skin that is being pickled, this is okay. I have left skins in the pickle solution for up to a couple of weeks, and I've heard of others who have left skins in the pickle much longer. If skins are left longer than the two twenty-four-hour periods—you can't get to the next step just yet and have no choice but to leave them—be certain to at least check on the pickle and regulate the pH. Should the pH rise above 3.0, add a small amount of acid, or you may experience problems later on.

Step 4: Degreasing the Skin

Once the pickle soak has been completed, the taxidermist must determine whether the skin being tanned should next be degreased. It may or may not need this step.

Degreasing methods may vary slightly. Some taxidermists neutralize the skin before degreasing (neutralizing is the next step, below). Others, including myself, choose to degrease while the skin is still in a pickled state, by depositing it into a degreaser bath. I feel this eliminates any problems which may occur after the neutralizing process. Most large mammals other than bears require very little to no degreasing whatsoever, so this step can be considered optional until you form an opinion as to which, if any, of the skins you work with will require degreasing.

As with acids and tans, numerous degreasers are available. Some taxidermists swear by Dawn dishwashing liquid as a degreasing agent. I personally use Dawn for nearly all my work with big game if I am tanning in-house or using dry preservative. Beyond this basic, mild degreaser, another commercial-grade degreaser that I have had experience with is called Epo-Grip Bloodout/Degreaser HD. Simply follow the directions that accompany the bottle and you should have no problem with this or any degreaser. A degreaser of any kind helps to break down soluble fats that may be within the skin's membrane. At this point they are easily washed away providing a cleaner skin that is easier to work with.

Step 5: Neutralizing the Skin

After the pickle bath and degreasing stages, you must neutralize the skin. Neutralizing is bypassed by some more experienced taxidermists, but for the beginner, neutralization should be considered mandatory. Neutralizing the skin simply raises its pH level to a neutral state, allowing it to accept the tannins that will be introduced during the final stage of the tanning process. Tannins are, in essence, artificial proteins that cushion the skin structure and further stabilize the skin to prevent decay.

To neutralize, begin by mixing two tablespoons of baking soda for each gallon of lukewarm water. The pH level for the

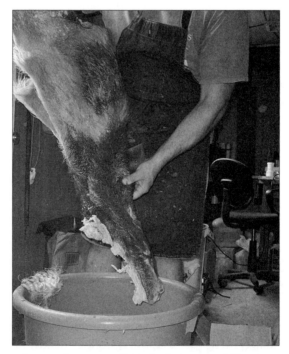

After degreasing a pelt, a neutralizing bath is a good idea because it stabilizes the pelt, prepping it for final stages of tanning.

neutralizer should be approximately 7.0. Should the pH turn out higher, simply add water, and if it is lower, add a small amount of baking soda, and then mix thoroughly and recheck. Do this until you reach a pH of 7.0.

Now deposit the pickled skin into the neutralizer. You may have to weigh the skin down as it will likely float (an effect of the pickling). After a soak of between fifteen and twenty minutes, remove the skin and immediately give it a thorough rinse.

Step 6: Applying the Tan

The last step is the actual tanning of the skin. I use the popular Knoblochs Liqua Tan as my primary in-shop tan, but there are other products available that work just as well. Other tanning products include Lutan-F and Bollman's tanning system.

Apply the tan to the entire flesh side of the skin. Now, fold the cape or life-size skin together, skin side to skin side, and roll it all up and place it into a freezer for later (the tan will actually soak in while in the freezer), or just let the folded-over skin sit for six to eight hours at room temperature.

Once the skin has been allowed to soak up the tan, I will place a small amount of Dawn dishwashing liquid into two gallons of water and quickly wash the skin. The tan will not wash out, but any excess oil will. Rinse the skin thoroughly and proceed with the mounting process.

Additionally, there are tans called *soak tans*. You can use these after all other stages of the tanning process have been completed. Submerge the skin in the soak tan to soak for an allotted amount of time, depending on the type or brand of tan. For someone who would like to use this method, rather than the tan-and-fold approach, I suggest Lutan-F. Numerous taxidermists have used this product for many years, and it has a good reputation for producing quality results. As with any product, follow the instructions carefully.

COMMERCIAL TANNERIES

A quality commercial tannery can often be of major help to the taxidermist. Notice I said *quality*. Talk with your fellow taxidermists and you will quickly weed out the problem companies. Granted, if you deal with a tannery long enough, you are likely to encounter a problem of some kind. But it is the frequency of these problems that you should be most concerned about. Also, although fully qualified tanneries are a tremendous asset to the taxidermist, they can't fix problems that are already beyond repair. This is where proper field care and prep work by the taxidermist plays an important role.

There are some taxidermists, both beginner and professional, who will choose to devote their time to the mounting process alone, and they will definitely require the services of a commercial tannery. If you don't have the time or space for the necessities of tanning, then commercial tanneries are ideal. Also, when first learning the mounting process, you will find that working with a properly cleaned, tanned, and degreased skin is much easier than trying to succeed with a barely passable skin of your own amateurish making. Trying to cover a manikin with a poorly preserved skin will only cause frustration and problems which will hinder an otherwise knowledgeable attempt.

After reading about all the details of this process, you might feel a bit overwhelmed. Don't worry about it. After many years in the taxidermy business, I have formed the opinion that nothing is always completely right—although some things can be *totally* wrong. There are some steps that must be done in a certain way, but otherwise, feel free to experiment. Develop your own tricks and customizations. I base a lot of my personal approach on the set of circumstances that I face with each given job. Customer demands and how well a customer has cared for a cape or animal in the field play a big part in the process. You, too, will soon begin to form your own opinions as to what approach to take, and when.

Throughout this book we will use a combination of the dry-preservative and tanning methods. For those attempting that first deer mount, I suggest using a dry-preserved skin. If you handle the process correctly, you should be able to enjoy the resulting mount for a long time. Then, as soon as you are comfortable using the dry-preservative method, give tanning a try. Soon you will begin to fully understand the pros and cons of each method, and you'll be able to choose the one that works best for you.

CHAPTER 7

Premounting Preparation

A ll finished mounts, whether a shoulder mount, life-size, or simply a lined rug, have the same requirements for completion: you must skin it, flesh it, preserve it, and then mount it. That is where the similarities end, however. You have probably read in a previous chapter that mounting a deer is the same as mounting a moose, and in a sense this is correct; the main difference is obviously the size. Nevertheless, you must understand that if you are not up to the task, a deer will try your patience, and your will. Furthermore, should you attempt to begin the learning process on an animal the size of an elk or larger, the effort will probably kick your butt and send you home crying to Momma.

The first time I approached a moose that I had taken in British Columbia, I was in awe. The sheer size of this animal was unbelievable, and, to beat all, my guide said it wasn't a very big moose. The body was bigger than any of the cattle I'd ever seen on my buddy's farm in North Carolina. Just to lift the moose's head was a chore. After the skinning process was complete, the unskinned head and cape tipped the scales at a weight very close to what most average, live whitetails weigh in my home state. Though I had mounted my share of large animals up to this point, they had always been brought in already skinned, salted, and with the rack removed. Though these projects seemed excessively large compared to the deer that I was used to, it was nothing like what you will experience firsthand

Even a small moose is still a moose. Beginning taxidermists do best starting with animals that are not very large.

should you ever have the opportunity to grab hold of a large bull moose, or even an elk lying in the field a couple of miles from your vehicle.

These statements aren't meant to deter you from eventually working with larger big-game animals. I simply want to let you know what you are up against should you take on a larger project. The key to success is preparation and knowledge, both of which you will gain when working with deer.

MANIKIN SELECTION

You should have already taken several key measurements of the animal that are pertinent for selecting the properly sized manikin. As long as the measurements correspond from the animal being mounted and the selected manikin, any pose can be chosen. The ultimate deciding factor is where the mount is to be placed after completion, or if any damage has been done to the skin in a particular area that needs to be hidden—this is covered later in this chapter.

Placement of the final mount is another main factor to consider when choosing a manikin. Nothing is more frustrating than completely mounting a trophy animal only to find that the only spot available to display it, or the particular spot that you had in mind, will not work for the manikin chosen. Once I mounted an elk with a left turn of its head, planning to display it in my home. Everything went well until I was ready to hang my prize. That was when I discovered there wasn't a single place in my home that would accommodate an animal the size of an elk mounted in a left turn. Had I mounted the elk in a *right* turn, I would have had a couple of placement options. The only choice I had was to do some rearranging and then compromise on my preferred area to hang my trophy. So keep this in mind, especially with large projects, and take measurements and make sketches of the intended area for display, if you can.

Materials Needed

This is the point at which everything begins to come together. Prior to mounting any animal, no matter the size, gather all required tools and parts needed to complete the job and organize them in a place where you can readily get a hold of them. You need to line up the manikin and skin with antlers or horns, and having a mounting stand for these items can be extremely helpful. You should also have at hand the following:

- adhesive
- artificial eyes
- clay—both generic and Critter Clay
- Bondo

- six to ten 2½-inch wood screws
- slot-cutting tool
- Speed Septum material, which is colored plastic material that corresponds with the appropriate color and texture of the interior of the nostrils
- lip-tucking or sculpting tool
- regulator needles
- ear opener
- Stout Ruffer or manikin scratcher
- latex gloves
- needle and thread
- hair-setting gel—which is very beneficial to taming unruly hair, and along seams

GETTING STARTED

Assuming that the preserved skin has been properly test-fitted and that all the necessary tools and items are gathered, it's time to attach the manikin to the mounting stand using three of the wood screws. (When working with a manikin larger than deer, use four or more heavy-duty screws when attaching it to the mounting stand.)

With the manikin positioned at a comfortable working height, use a slot-cutting tool to cut the lip slot as well as the tear duct slots. During the learning stages you will achieve the best results by following the original lip lines and tear ducts that are already preimposed on the manikin. After you gain some experience and have studied a good deal of reference material, you can choose to alter these lines slightly. For best results when cutting the lip line, position the slot-cutting tool at an approximate 45-degree angle. In the tear duct areas, cut both sides to match, in both the shape and angle of the cut. Continue by shaping the interior of each nostril using a Dremel

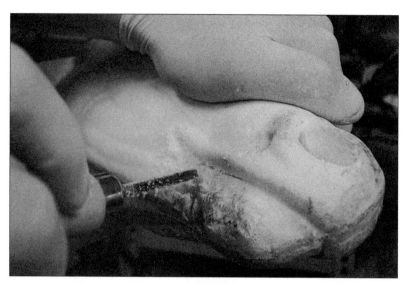

The prepressed lines on a manikin are a good guide for your slot cutter, but you can customize the shape as needed.

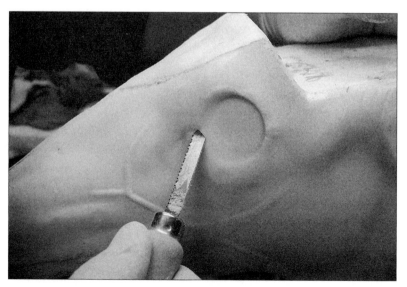

Take care to make the tear ducts the same size, so go slow with your slot cutter, checking each side.

tool, with a bit specially designed to shape and cut. A small drill bit works exceptionally well for shaping.

To achieve the best results, carefully examine reference photos of the nostril area of a live deer. It is also helpful to study precast artificial noses, some of which are created to replace the original manikin nose, while others are for reference purposes only. The reference type generally can be taken apart in sections to allow for the examination of each nostril all the way up into its interior. Once you have an appropriate shape in mind, work slowly using the Dremel tool, and don't remove too much material at any one time. Proceed with careful, very thin slices. I open the nostrils to a point slightly smaller than what might be exact, because you'll be surprised at how large the nostrils can appear once the skin is positioned and properly dried.

Once you have achieved a nostril shape that is very close to the reference you are using, make any final adjustments using a sculpting tool. For most commercial mounts, you should clear a

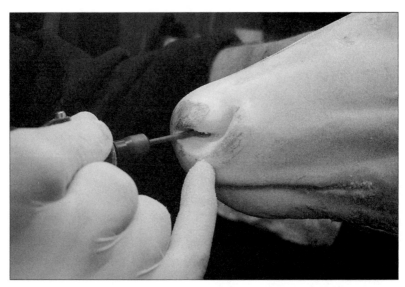

Leave the manikin nostrils a bit smaller than seems right—they'll look wide enough when done.

path from one nostril to the other through the interior wall. This will allow the placement of a Speed Septum on each side which will simulate the color and texture of the interior of a deer's nose. Placement of a septum will also reduce the amount of finish work that must be done to complete the interior of the nose. These septums come in different sizes and can be used on all big game. Speed Septum kits contain septums for ten animals, and, usually, a tool for cutting an appropriately shaped slot.

Finish the initial manikin preparation by scratching its entire surface area to remove the residual layer of release agent that all manufacturers spray on their molds. (This release agent prevents the foam body material from sticking to the mold, and it must be removed in order for the adhesive to work properly.) Several tools are available for this task, but as mentioned, I have found that the Stout Ruffer seems to work much better than many of the other tools available. If this scratching or roughing of the manikin surface isn't done properly, the cape

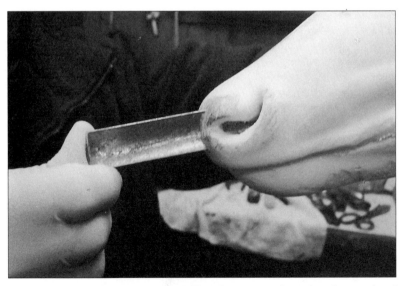

With a septum-insertion tool, you'll make a curved cut on the inside of each nostril by pushing through the nose tip.

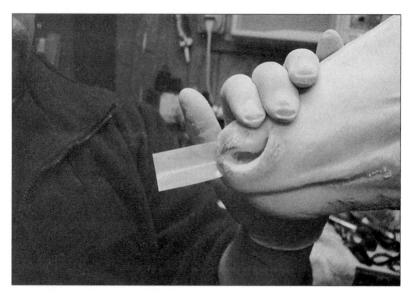

The septum insert goes into the curved cut, thus creating a realistic interior for the nostrils.

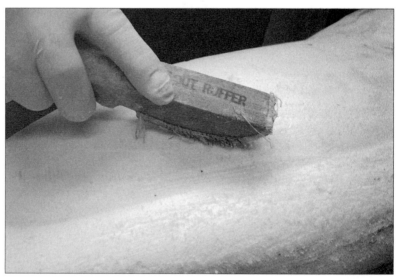

Use a Stout Ruffer to remove the layer of "release agent" from the body of the manikin before mounting.

will not adhere adequately to the manikin, and poor adhesion can lead to drumming.

Your next step is to attach the antlers to the manikin. To do this, take the antlers—which are still attached to the skull plate, all in one unit—in hand and place them onto the flat area on the rear portion of the head area. Make certain the skull plate fits appropriately and doesn't stand above the foam of the manikin. If this occurs, trim off small amounts of each side until the skull plate fits appropriately. Also, you need to ensure that the antlers are protruding from the manikin at an appropriate angle. (For the positioning of the antlers to be exact, measure from the tip of each main beam to the center of the nose, prior to skinning, and then reposition accordingly when attaching them.)

Once the skull plate is positioned properly, drill two ¼-inch holes near the front of the skull plate, and then an additional hole in the center of the rear of the skull plate. You'll be screw-

Before attaching the skull plate to the manikin, check its fit and also be sure the antlers sit at the proper angle.

ing the plate in place soon. To finish preparing the skull plate for attachment, mix an appropriate amount of Bondo and partially fill the skull plate, making certain that the entire edge of the plate has a small amount of Bondo in place. Place the antlers and skull plate back into their intended position. If trimmed properly, the skull plate should sit perfectly in this area. Initially, you might have to hold the rack in place by hand as the Bondo hardens; then, once the Bondo has set significantly, you can insert the screws and lightly tighten them. Soon after the Bondo begins to harden, trim off any excess that may be protruding from the edges of the skull plate.

If the cape at hand has a full-length cut, leave the skull plate in place with the antlers, and finish shaping the top of the skull by adding a small amount of clay to the areas that once had muscle tissue attached to them. You'll be able to pull the cape itself over the manikin with the antlers in place. But if the cape you are using has a short Y-incision, when the Bondo beneath the skull plate is firm, you will need to remove the

Add enough Bondo to fill the skull plate.

Hold the antlers steady as the Bondo dries so that they don't list to one side.

screws and then knock the plate and antlers free from the manikin using the palm of your hand (the Bondo will come free of the manikin). In this situation, you will permanently attach the antlers once the cape has been pulled onto the manikin during the final mounting stages.

LIFE-SIZE MANIKIN PREP

When preparing a life-size manikin, follow all of the steps described above, and then continue with the body. Obviously the remainder of the manikin must be roughed, but in my opinion, the body of the animal isn't nearly as critical as the head, neck, and shoulder area, unless you're entering a mount into a competition. This is generally due to the fact that the head and neck present a great number of details that must be re-created accurately.

After completely roughing the body, you might need to cut relief slots under the armpits and between the rear legs. This should be done on all manikins, but it is mandatory for those with extreme leg angles, such as those manikins set in running and bedded poses. I make such cuts using a reciprocating saw, and I notch out between the legs until there is enough room to allow any excess skin to slide into place. To understand this better, allow your arms to hang by your sides. Notice that your skin-to-skin contact may extend from your armpit halfway to the elbow; the same is true with animals. However, to allow for easier removal of the manikin from the mold, the manufacturers fill in these limb-to-body interfaces. Since you have a skin that can cover more surface area than such a pose offers, you must simply remove this small amount of material to prevent the skin from bunching in these areas. Complete the life-size manikin preparation by using a knife to remove a small amount of manikin material—about the size of a golf ball—at what would be the anal opening. This will later be filled with clay (which will provide a better working medium for tucking the anal skin), thus presenting a more lifelike appearance, as is the case with a running white-tailed deer where the tail is carried high.

EYE SCULPTING

You should insert and model the eyes before you apply any adhesive to the manikin to mount the skin. This is because you will need to work on the eye socket a bit, and you can't do this with the skin in place.

The following section details the eye work required for a white-tailed deer, the species that probably makes up more than 70 percent of all starting projects (as well as future projects) for the average taxidermist. Eye techniques for other big game will be very similar, with only minute changes, and I detail these differences in chapter 9.

Cutting a small divot in the eye socket creates more surface area for securing the eye.

To begin, use a sculpting tool to dig out a divot in the center of the eye slot. This will help hold the artificial eye securely in place. Continue by taking a small amount of Critter Clay, about the size of a marble, and forming a cone shape. Affix the base of this cone into the convex back side of the eye. At this point, make certain that the manikin backboard is at a right angle to the floor, or parallel to an adjacent wall. This will help set the eye pupils at the appropriate angle, which for all big-game animals is almost perfectly parallel to the ground, no matter the pose.

While some artificial eyes for animals such as elk and buffalo are light in color and the pupil is easily visible, most artificial deer eyes are very dark. For easier viewing, use a flashlight to look into the eye, noticing the elongated pupil. Now, simply insert the eye with the pupil parallel to the floor. Push the eye until it seats at the bottom of the eye pocket and continue with the opposite side in the same manner.

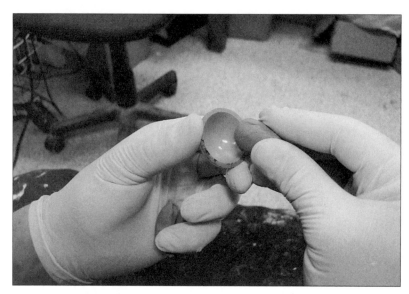

Inserting clay into the hollow, convex eye gives it cushioning and more surface area for adhering to the socket.

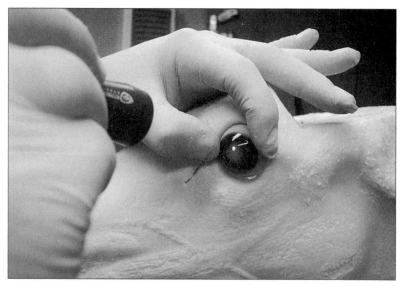

With darker eyes, such as those for deer, use a flashlight to see the pupil and set the eyes with the pupils parallel to the ground.

Some eyes that are very anatomically correct will have a front and rear of the eye. To distinguish these eyes from the basic artificial eye, lay them flat on a table and take notice of whether the eye has a consistent roundness (like a bobber or a ball), or whether the eye seems to slant slightly to one side. If the eye you are using does have a slant, make sure it's always positioned toward the nose of the mount. To make things simple, I suggest using the most basic eye possible. A Tohickon Brite-Tech eye, available at Research Mannikins is ideal for commercial mounts, as well as for learning purposes, and there is no wrong way to insert this eye, as long as the pupil is parallel to the floor.

After inserting each eye, roll a golf ball–sized portion of clay into a shape that is slightly larger than a pencil. Keep in mind when preparing to model the eyes that with most modern manikins, very little clay will be needed because much of the brow has already been presculpted. Most taxidermists agree that having too little clay is much better than having too much. Once you work the clay ball into the appropriate shape, begin mashing one end flat. Continue mashing along the roll for a couple of inches, then pinch the end slightly and begin to form a curved, pointed end shaped kind of like a bear claw. (Experience will soon teach you exactly how to shape the end of this clay edge that you are forming).

With the clay shaped, take the pointed, downward end of the mashed strip and attach it in the front corner of the artificial eye. This would be just forward of the eye in the depression that sits between the tear duct and the eye. Lay the flattened clay strip along the top edge of the eye, with the edge of the strip covering the eyeball perhaps an eighth of an inch—a distance that should coincide with your reference photos—and then continue along the top of the eye, very gradually falling off to the rear of the eye. Now take the clay and again roll out a small portion between your hands, this time slightly smaller than the one before, but also with a pointed end. Again, starting

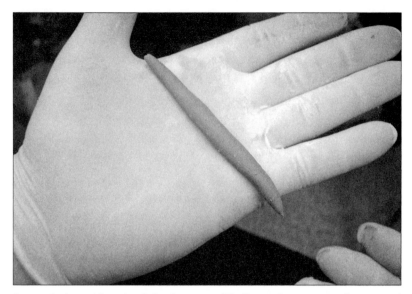

A pencil-shaped length of clay from a golf ball–sized amount is all you need to sculpt around the deer's eyes.

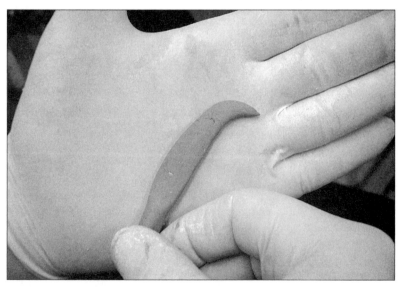

Mash the clay pencil flat, and create one pointed, slightly curved end to fit into the front corner of the eye socket.

at the front of the eye, insert the point of the small clay roll into the tiny crack between the eye and the manikin; then, slowly apply the flattened clay strip along the bottom of the eye, slowly dropping rearward, until the rear third of the eye has been reached. Then, carefully roll up the rear of the eye until you meet the clay from the upper lid.

Now you must apply a heavier forward brow, and a small amount of clay on each side of the tear duct to help with a smooth transition in the tear duct area. To form the top-forward brow, again roll the clay ball into a shape slightly larger than a pencil, flatten it, and work a flattened end to a shallow point. Take the shaped clay and secure the point nearly over the top of the initial upper-brow attachment point. Then, gradually attach the clay along the front of the eye, overlapping the first clay strip to the high point of the eyebrow, and then angle off the initial clay application, allowing about a quarter-inch of the first clay strip to be visible. Keep this amount of exposed underlying

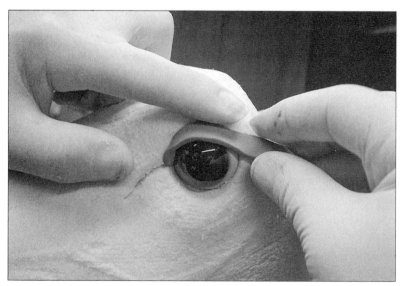

Create the flesh of the eyebrow by drawing the clay over the top of the eyeball, coming down about an eighth of an inch over the eye.

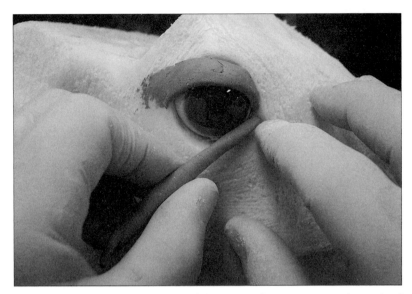

Do the same for the lower edge of the eye socket, connecting the ends of the clay strips at the rear corner.

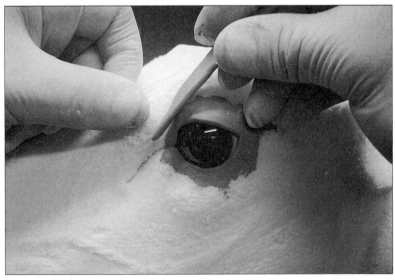

To complete both eyes, add one last bit of clay over the first eyebrow layer and blend it in to the clay underneath.

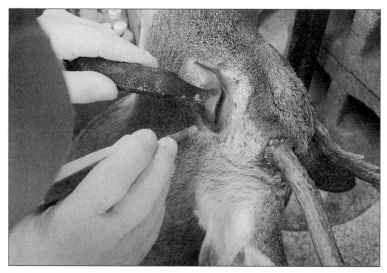

Eye-set tools are a big help to getting consistent shapes for eye sockets.

clay very uniform in width from the high point of the brow to the rear. Once you reach the rear of the eyebrow, go back and taper this top strip until it is blended fully into the underlying clay, so you can't tell that two separate clay applications exist in the same spot. Repeat this whole process on the opposite eye, and the modeling of the eyes will be complete.

As mentioned previously, developing the ability to do this flawlessly will take time and practice. To help with those initial attempts, I highly recommend using a Quick-Set Eye Tool, which is an implement designed to provide a general pattern for brow and eyelid sculpting. This is a great tool that can help even the experienced taxidermist maintain a consistent shape.

SHAPING AND FORMING THE EARS

Shaping the ears of most big-game animals is very similar to dealing with the eyes in the sense that each ear must be inverted to the edge. Then, once the cape has been preserved with either dry preservative or a tan, an ear liner or Bondo must be inserted into the ear to hold its natural shape; otherwise, the ear would curl upon drying. Many knowledgeable taxidermists agree that Bondo works exceptionally well for commercial work, as it easily accommodates deformed or split ears. Bondo is also relatively inexpensive and readily available. Though the ears of individual animals will vary in shape and size, preparation will be virtually the same.

Once the ears are turned completely, use a knife to score the cartilage, which is the much thicker side of each ear. Be careful not to cut through the skin while scoring the cartilage. Be sure to score from top to bottom and left to right, forming a pattern similar to that of a checkerboard. This will serve to weaken the cartilage as it completes the drying process. Though weakening of the ear cartilage isn't mandatory, without doing so the ears can sometimes curl, creating an unnatural appearance.

Once the ears are scored, mix a small amount of Bondo with the hardener and insert it into each ear. (Using an amount

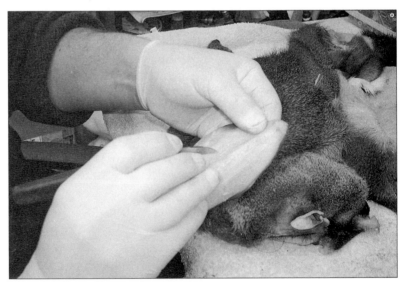

Ears sometimes curl while drying, so prevent that by scoring their cartilage with a scalpel or knife.

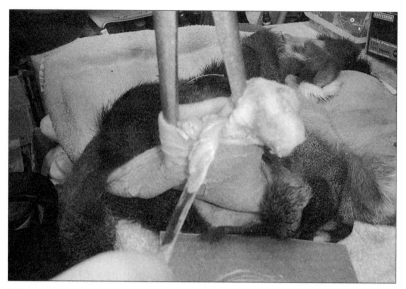

Fill dried ears with just enough Bondo to give them sufficient shape.

of hardener that is smaller than usual will allow a much longer working time.) For medium deer-sized ears, begin with about two tablespoons of Bondo for each ear. You can very easily overstuff the ears, so once you think you have almost enough in an ear, stop filling and begin to slowly shape the ear with your fingers. With the cartilage still attached, the ear will tend to hold a shape very close to that of a live deer. Only a small amount of shaping will be needed to evenly distribute the Bondo. Also, ear forms are available for several species. You insert the ear into the form after filling the ear with Bondo, and the form acts to properly shape each ear. Personally, I insert the Bondo, slowly work and shape the ear by hand, and then, when the shape and thickness is very near to what I want, I allow the head area of the skin to hang off the edge of a table. This is done by simply allowing the weight of the skin behind the neck area to lay on a table, and the head skin is allowed to hang towards the floor. If the weight of the skin isn't sufficient to hold the skin on the table once the head is allowed to hang from the side, position a small amount of weight on the skin to prevent it from sliding off the table. A large Bondo can or bag of clay is ideal for this. By freeing the ear from the pull of gravity by laying it against a flat surface, this allows the ear to take a shape that is very close to being natural. Then, once the Bondo begins to thicken—keep track of this by observing any unused portion—again pick up the ear and slowly, but more firmly, make certain that the ear is in the desired shape.

Preparing the ears in this manner is a relatively simple procedure, but for those who aren't used to working with Bondo, it can be messy. You will need some practice to get this procedure down pat, but after numerous attempts, it will become very easy to complete—much easier, in my opinion, than removing the cartilage and trimming an ear liner. If, however, the first few attempts go terribly awry, don't attempt to remove the Bondo while it remains in a creamy consistency. Once the Bondo reaches the initial hardening stages, it can then be easily removed from within the ear as well as the surrounding hair, allowing you to start over.

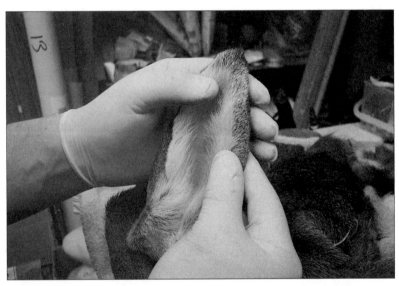

Check the ear as the Bondo dries inside to make sure that it keeps the proper shape.

FINAL MANIKIN PREP

Before moving to the last step of manikin preparation, make certain that all materials are ready and close by, because once you begin this last step, you must continue the mounting process until it is complete. It's "all in" after this.

Next comes the adhesive application. A general adhesive applied to the body—up to the neck area on a life-size manikin, and the neck-and-shoulder area for a shoulder mount—is generally adequate. For the head, as well as for any sharp depressions in the neck, shoulder, or body area, many taxidermists use an epoxy-based adhesive. Using an epoxy adhesive will lock down the skin much more quickly and will prevent it from shifting during the drying process. Using an epoxy-based adhesive for these areas isn't mandatory; in fact, many taxidermists will use a dextrin-based hide paste, manipulating the skin slightly each day until the paste has completely dried.

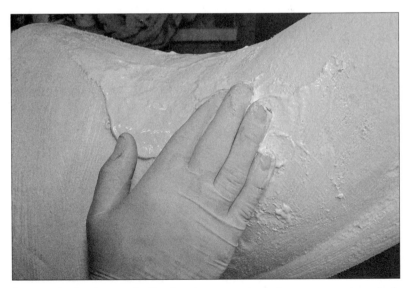

A general adhesive works fine for the mount body, but an epoxy-based adhesive is better in areas of irregular surfaces.

For your first few mounts, you might want to use a regular adhesive on the entire manikin, rather than an epoxy-based one. Epoxies dry quickly and offer no pardon to the beginner who may need more time to complete the mounting process. Applying the adhesive is fairly simple, and you will develop tricks along the way to help prevent getting adhesive onto the fur, which is the main mistake beginners make. If any adhesive gets onto the hair, it can be removed using a lacquer thinner, glass cleaner, or sometimes, just plain water, but having to do so just creates more work for the taxidermist and lengthens the time it takes to complete your project.

To avoid these problems, apply the adhesive to within just a few inches of where the skin will come together on each side—that is, along the seam on the back of the head for V-cuts; along the back for a full-length Y-cut on a shoulder manikin; and the full length of the body for a life-size mount. Use a few regulator needles or pins to attach the skin to these places on the manikin where there is no adhesive. Then, as you sew the skin, remove these attachment points one at a time. This can significantly decrease the risk of the hair being constantly dragged through the adhesive as you begin the sewing process, after the major portion of the skin has been adhered to the manikin.

As mentioned earlier in this chapter, all mounts, no matter what the finished product is destined to be, will begin in the same manner. All techniques described here will transfer from one big-game animal to the next, with the only difference being the size of the manikin, along with reference material, and the skin and antlers or horns particular for each mount. Further procedures, both universal and individualized—such as the placement and sculpting of the eye—will be documented in each of the following chapters that chart the mount to completion.

CHAPTER 8

The Classic Deer Shoulder Mount

Without a doubt, a shoulder mount of a deer should be a big-game taxidermist's initial project. There are many reasons for this suggestion, and for those who may think I am being a bit too restrictive, I will explain. Elk are big, and moose are bigger. Bear are nasty and greasy, and so are wild hogs. Antelope are extremely thin-skinned and fragile, and critters such as sheep and goats are much too difficult to obtain; the cape of either one of them comes with a price tag that few taxidermists can pay without reservations.

That leaves us with our good old reliable deer—and why not? Many people hunt and desire a trophy deer, and the shoulder-mount whitetail is a true American classic. Deer skin is tough, but not too thick, and the species isn't too large and is generally plentiful—especially for those living in whitetail country. Simply put, deer make the perfect starter project.

Remember, because this is an initial attempt, you should avoid using a once-in-a-lifetime trophy animal, or even a really nice buck. I'm sure that you would like to mount a prized trophy as quickly as possible, but the best advice for the beginner is to set aside a prized animal in the freezer until you have a bit of experience under your belt. Your first mount will look nothing like your fifth—or even your twenty-fifth, for that matter—

Given the huge popularity of deer, most working taxidermists will spend the bulk of their time preparing deer mounts.

because if you put forth the necessary effort, the work that you produce will continue to evolve and improve.

To get started, take advantage of a doe that a hunting partner may have taken for meat, or utilize a management buck. Both of these can make great mounts. As a matter of fact, one of the most interesting pieces of work I've ever seen at a taxidermy competition was a pedestal-mounted button buck. The deer appeared to be nibbling on an ear of corn, and the work was unbelievable. After speaking to the taxidermist, I found that he had salvaged the small buck from alongside a highway after seeing a vehicle he had been following hit the animal. Though the circumstances were less than desirable, at least the taxidermist had the good sense to salvage the skin for an upcoming project, which by the way, won him a blue ribbon. So keep in mind that not all masterpieces are monster bucks or very rare animals.

For the mounting process I'll discuss in this chapter, my comments refer to a V-cut deer cape that has been preserved using dry preservative. The manikin I used is a semi-sneak First Honest Whitetail from Research Mannikins. The eyes are 32-millimeter Joe Meder IQ eyes. The adhesive is latex-based, and the clay used for fill-in around the base of the skull is just bulk clay, but the clay used around the eyes, as described in the previous chapter on premounting preparation, is Critter Clay. I used Critter Clay during the mounting process to help reduce shrinkage in critical areas. For sewing, I used a large S-needle and an artificial sinew for thread.

Now that all of the particulars are out of the way, let's get started.

MOUNTING PROCESS

If you have followed the directions from each previous chapter for your shoulder-mount deer, all that is left are the actual steps that complete the mounting process. When you last dealt with the cape, you inserted Bondo into the ears and allowed it to harden. If excess Bondo extends beyond the base of the ear, where the muscle tissue of the ear base was once attached, you must remove it. Any excess Bondo should break free easily. Doing so while the Bondo is pliable is much easier, but you can break off Bondo at almost any stage.

Finish the ears by filling the interior of the ear base area with a portion of generic clay, slightly larger than a golf ball, for each ear. This is to fill in the area where muscle tissue was previously attached to the ear base. To get a good idea of how this clay should be shaped, look closely at the musculature of an ear base during the skinning process. For additional reference, study ear base casts—which are commercially available for reference—and live photos. A beginner will often form an ear base that is too large, which generally pushes the ear too far away from the head. To prevent this, use only the suggested amount of clay for each ear base—approximately the size of a golf ball on smallish ear bases, and roughly 30 percent larger for the largest ear bases. Make certain you insert the clay fully, and blend it gradually to the cartilage of the ear.

At this point the cape should be ready to pull onto the prepped manikin, and if you haven't already done so, apply a thin coat of adhesive to the entire manikin. To prevent adhesive from contaminating the hair, invert the cape halfway, with the shoulder area pulled forward over the head and face of the cape, so the skin of the cape has basically been doubled over and the hair side sandwiched between the two sides of the fold.

Then, stand behind the manikin and position the cape so that you can pull it onto the manikin, pulling it rearward, and making sure to locate the ears atop the head and position the brisket in the bottom center of the manikin. Pulling the cape onto the manikin in this manner will generally allow most areas

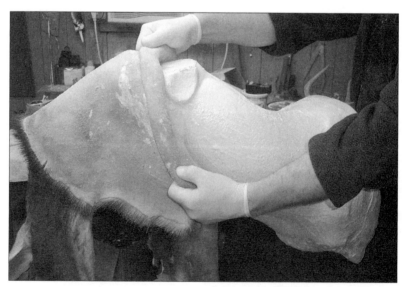

While mounting the cape, be extra careful not to get adhesive on the fur.

of the cape to match up with the corresponding areas of the manikin without too much repositioning. This means that the eyes of the cape will be near the artificial eyes that have been installed into the manikin, and also the shoulder areas will fall into their appropriate places, and so on and so forth. Imagine this step as if you're reaching around a child to wrap him or her in a blanket from head to toe, touching only one side of the blanket to the child.

At this point you should understand that there is no particular order in which to complete the remaining steps. Personal preference will dictate this. Some taxidermists will continue the mounting process by modeling the face and sewing any seams, and then they will arrange the skin into its appropriate position before finishing the mount by stapling the cape to the back of the manikin. What follows is my preferred method, after several years of experience.

Once the cape is pulled onto the manikin and the skin is positioned according to the hair patterns and reference, I use a staple gun to secure the excess skin onto the back side of the manikin to prevent the shoulders and brisket area from getting loose and possibly doubling over and touching the adhesive. Inserting just a few staples will allow easy detachment of the skin in this area should you need to reposition it once you have completed the remaining steps of the mounting process. Return to the back of the manikin and permanently anchor the cape with additional staples, and then trim any excess skin.

With the skin anchored onto the backboard, spread open the incision on top of the head and reinsert the skull plate that you had positioned earlier onto a bed of Bondo, assuming you're using a short Y-cut (as I almost always do). After placing the skull plate into the appropriate position, insert and tighten the three 2½-inch wood screws that you used to anchor the skull plate. Continue by using generic clay to replace any muscle tissue that may have been removed along the edge of the

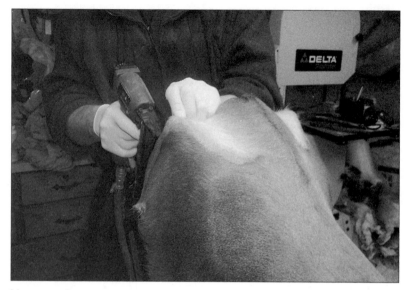

Use a staple gun to secure any excess skin to the flat back of a shoulder-mount manikin.

skull plate during the skinning process. I sometimes add a very thin layer of clay onto the surface of the skull plate to help conceal any seams. The seams can be pressed into the soft substance below, alleviating any ridges that might arise atop an otherwise hard surface. In addition, before closing up the Y-seam, take a small portion of clay and roll it into the shape of a small pencil. Wrap this roll around the skull plate, just under each antler burr. Placing a small roll of clay in this area will help to adhere the skin tightly to the skull pedicle around the base of the antler burr.

With all clay in place, anchor each side of the skin with a regulator needle in order to hold the skin in position while the sewing process is completed. Sew the seam using a baseball stitch—insert the needle on the skin side; pull upward through the hair, and then cross over to the opposing side; once again, insert the needle into the skin side and out the hair side, similar

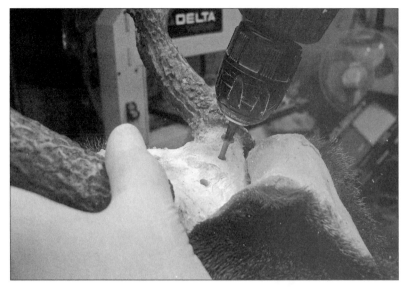

Once you have the cape in place, replace the skull plate and antlers, anchoring the plate with wood screws.

Where necessary, build up the base of the antlers or the edges of the skull plate with a small amount of clay.

to forming a figure eight. Begin sewing at the base of one antler, making certain that all stitches are very tight to prevent the seams from widening during the drying process. Once one leg of the Y is complete, tie off the stitch and repeat, beginning on the opposite antler base. But this time, continue stitching until the entire seam is fully closed, and then tie off the stitch and press the seam down until it is flat against the manikin. At this point, make certain that all stitching is tight, and move on to modeling the face.

Modeling the Face

Use a Stout Ruffer or a regulator needle to move the skin into position on the face. The fresh adhesive should allow the skin to glide easily along the surface of the manikin. Work the eyes, nose, and throat patches into proper position before continuing.

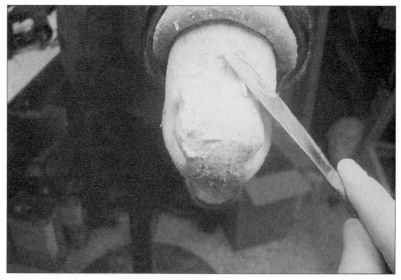

The slipperiness of the adhesive should allow you to move the skin around the face and into position relatively easily.

With all skin areas appropriately placed, use a lip-tucking or sculpting tool to tuck the skin of each nostril into the nostrils of the manikin. Make certain that the small white hairs of the nostril area are visible only inside the nostrils and that they don't extend onto the nose pad area. Once the nose is positioned and the nostrils inserted, continue by turning the mount upside down, which will allow easier access to the lip line.

Begin at the rear corner of one side of the lip line and tuck the skin of the bottom lip. Tuck only an inch or so of the bottom lip from this rear corner, and then begin tucking the top lip. Try to do this without contaminating any hair with the underlying adhesive. Once you have evenly tucked both the top and bottom lips, repeat this on the opposite side. With the lip line tucked in each corner (just a small amount), repeat the tucking procedure under the nose area. Again, tuck the bottom lip and then the top, doing this from one edge of the nose pad to the other.

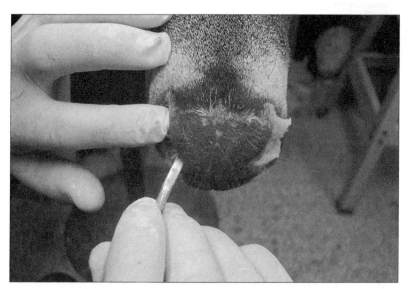

You can tuck the interior flesh of the nose into the nostrils with a sculpting tool.

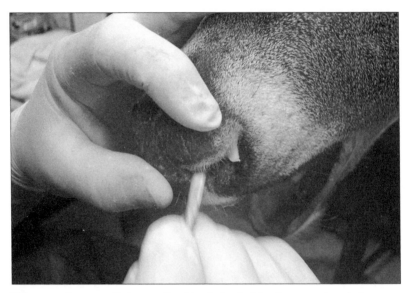

When you've got all the small white hairs inside the nostril and the nose pad is tight, you've fit the nose.

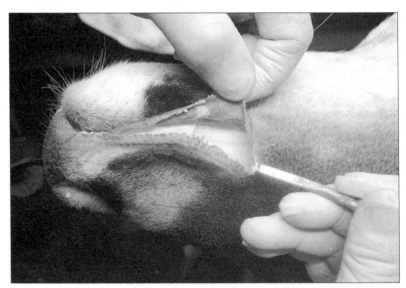

Begin tucking the lower and upper lip from the corner of the mouth.

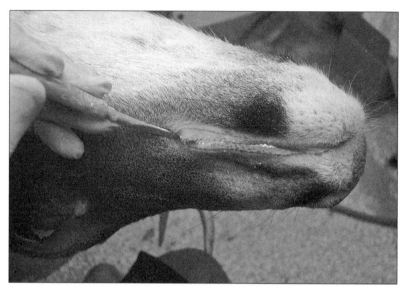

You need to tuck only about an inch of skin into the lip line.

You will probably have excess skin along the lip line on each side of the face, due to the naturally elastic nature of the skin and the effects of skinning and fleshing. To combat this slack, begin tucking the lip line once again in the same manner as before, but this time, tuck between the nose and the rear corner of the mouth. By tucking forward to the nose area, as well as rearward to the corner of the mouth, this slack will slowly be taken out. Consult your reference material frequently as a guideline and pay close attention to hair patterns along the edge of the upper lip, lower lip, the rear corner of the mouth, and the area just under the nose.

To model the eye, insert a sculpting tool into the eye opening and pull both the top and bottom eyelid away from the manikin. After making certain that both the front and rear corner of the eye, as well as the top and bottom eyelids, are appropriately positioned, carefully begin tucking the tear duct into the small slot cut in the manikin, extending from the front corner of the eye. Tuck all the bare skin into this slot, making

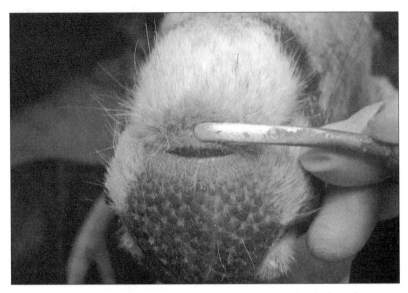

Work out any slack in the lip line by tucking excess skin below the nose, and at the corners of the mouth.

sure that the tear duct area closely resembles that of your reference. If you positioned clay alongside this slot during the initial modeling process of the eye, smooth it gently toward the interior of the tear duct. The primary goal here is to offer a smooth, flowing appearance that doesn't have any odd edges.

Next, use the sculpting tool to pull the clay away from the eye to allow room to tuck the small portion of skin extending past the eyelid. This is most easily done by simply placing the sculpting tool against the artificial eye and running it along the clay line, just deep enough to form a small void for this skin to be inserted. Then begin tucking the skin, starting from the front corner and working along the top of the eye to the back corner, then again from the front corner along the bottom of the eye, until the skin around the eye has been completely tucked into place. To soften the eye area as well as the tear duct, use a medium-sized round paintbrush to gently push into place the tissues in these areas.

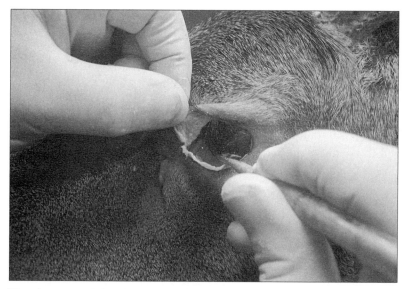

The skin around the eyes calls for precise, neat tucking to account for the often elastic nature of the skin in this area.

If available, use the Quick-Set Eye Tool to achieve a more realistic shape of the eye. Insert the tool into the eye area and shape the surrounding skin accordingly. Because the eyes play a major role in bringing a mount to life, use close-up reference photos as you re-create the entire eye area. To add some realism, you may wish to form a very small crease from the front corner of the eye along the top edge, with this crease tapering off as the rear third of the eye is reached. After both eyes and tear ducts are smooth in appearance and appropriately shaped, you will turn to your last area to position: the ears.

Technically, there is no wrong position in which to place the ears, as most live deer can hold their ears in a multitude of positions—alert, sagging, and twitching back and forth uniformly and independently, to name a few. So you can position the ears at your discretion. I generally tend to place both ears in a halfway-back position. This is to simulate a relaxed, semi-alert deer—which is the mood that I feel deer are in a majority of the time. To get the ears into this position, gently grasp the ear near the base and insert a thumb into the inner ear. Now, place the ear base at an appropriate position—most manikins have ear placement indentations near the rear of the head to help with ear base attachment and positioning. With the ear at an appropriate angle and position, and oriented toward the correct indentation on the manikin, push the ear firmly but carefully onto the manikin. If done properly, the ear should hold its position and the angle at which it extends from the head. If not, try to position the ear base once again. If problems with this persist, insert a 12- to 14-inch length of 10-gauge wire into the ear base to anchor the ear firmly in place.

Lastly, cut two small, thin pieces of cardboard and tack them firmly into the manikin in the armpit areas, wedging them into the tight inner seam. This will eliminate any drumming that might occur in the armpit, as often happens due to the tight angle of the forelimb and body. In addition, use your fingers to

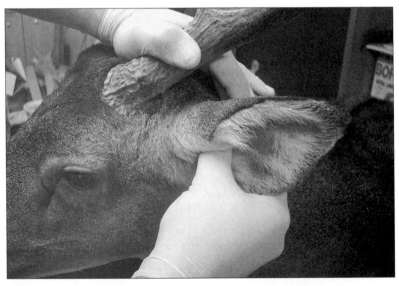

Keep in mind that a deer reveals a lot about its disposition with its ears, and they should match its body language and facial expression.

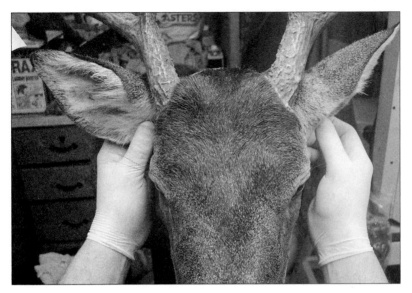

Most manikins come with ear placement indicators—you can feel them through the cape.

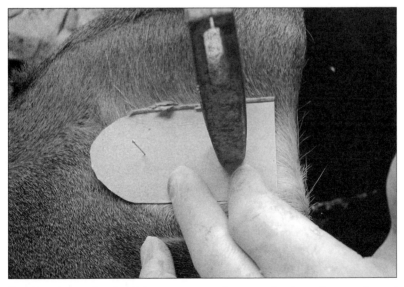

Prevent drumming in tight corners and seams by inserting cardboard pieces that will keep the skin in place.

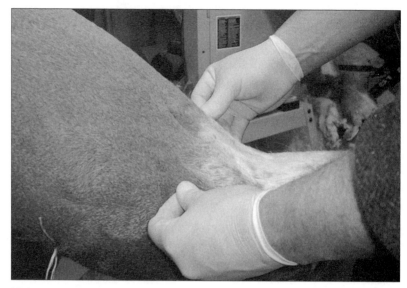

Make sure that the skin adheres closely to bodily details on the manikin, such as muscle edges and veins.

press the skin into any crease or depression that may exist on the manikin; these creases are generally sculpted onto the manikin to show muscle definition.

With all areas properly positioned, the mounting process is complete. However, a few additional steps must be taken to ensure that the mount dries properly. First, inspect the mount from nose to tail to make certain that all the steps have been completed properly and that all areas are appropriately positioned. Again, do this according to your reference material. Lightly mist the lip line, nose pad, eyes, and tear ducts with a glass cleaner or plain water, and then use a round medium paintbrush to make certain that all these areas are clean of any contaminants.

Continue by using a sculpting tool to push a plastic sheeting into each nostril to help anchor the nostril skin to the interior of the manikin nostril—plastic grocery bags from a grocery store are ideal for this. Use cardboard with several straight pins

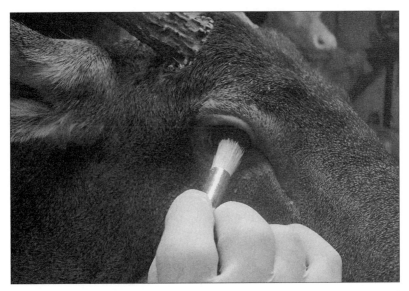

You can use soft paint and makeup brushes to clean up detailed surfaces of the mount, like the eyes and nose.

Plastic sheeting or a plastic shopping bag gently stuffed into the nostrils will help them keep shape as the mount dries.

inserted through to tack down any unruly hair or skin area that may be pulling away from the manikin. If the ears appear to be holding a proper position without drooping, it may not be necessary to use any support, but should the ears appear to have moved from the original positioning, reach for the 10-gauge wire and cut two 12- to 14-inch lengths to insert through the ear bases and into the manikin. This ensures that the ears will dry in the desired position. One last step is to use a hair-setting gel to lock down the hair along the back of the head and neck where any seams may be located.

Finally, go take a break—a long break. Return after allowing your mind and body to rest, and then take another look, making some tweaks if necessary. At this point, don't judge your work too harshly. If you are happy, great; if not, keep in mind that this isn't your last mount, and your work will improve with time.

CHAPTER 9

Antelope and Elk Shoulder Mounts

W hile white-tailed deer make up the mainstay of big-game taxidermy, there are plenty of other animals out there. For the purposes of this book, we're going to round out the discussion with antelope and elk, two other highly popular trophy species, especially if you live in the West.

These are two good species for the beginner to consider after gaining experience with the initial deer mounts. The antelope is

Western taxidermists will spend almost as much time on antelope as they will on deer mounts.

deer-sized, but has some interesting and unique features that require specific attention. As for an elk, its sheer size and the weight of its rack make it a major task for the amateur. The taxidermist who in her first couple of years produces near competition-worthy elk is really making progress.

Most people who have seen pronghorn in portions of western North America find these hoofed creatures uniquely beautiful. More commonly known as antelope (even though they aren't *true* antelopes), pronghorn have become symbolic of the high plains of many western states, with Wyoming possibly being the pronghorn capital of the world. Pronghorn have been known to reach speeds of sixty miles per hour while running, and researchers believe the animal's eyesight is equal to that of a person looking through 8X binoculars. They are also the only horned animal in the world that sheds and regrows its horn sheaths each year. Getting close to a pronghorn for a rifle shot isn't easy, and most shots are taken at significantly longer distances than shots for deer. So the hunter who comes home with a trophy pronghorn has every right to look forward to a very special mount.

Pronghorn easily number among the three or four most popular big-game mounts in North America. The taxidermist can handle them in much the same manner as deer, but there are some antelope-specific taxidermy issues that will be highlighted in this chapter.

Special Considerations for the Pronghorn

One major difference between pronghorn and deer is evident during the skinning process. You should skin a pronghorn using a full-length T-incision. The reason for this is primarily because of the smaller size of the neck and the larger size of the head, as compared to a deer, both of which require a longer-than-normal T-incision anyway. Also, pronghorn hair tends to be more fragile than that of a deer, and inverting the cape (as is necessary with a Y-cut) could damage the hair. I believe that the T-cut is much easier to use when cutting between and around the horns of a pronghorn. This cut also seems to follow the pronghorn hair pattern much better.

Another item you should remember when skinning and fleshing a pronghorn is that the skin is much thinner and the hair is hollow, qualities that allow the pelt to more readily soak up fluids, blood in particular. So skin carefully and avoid contaminating the hair with any blood or other bodily fluids that could permanently stain the hair.

To skin a pronghorn buck, cut the skin around the base of each horn. To locate the appropriate area to make this cut, follow the horn down its hard surface until you reach the skin, and cut around this junction until the skin is no longer connected to the horn. Finish the skinning process by cutting from one horn to another in a straight line. Then at a halfway point between the two horns, begin making the cut that will course along the center of the back. Both buck and doe pronghorn have horns, and both will be prepped in the same manner.

One additional area of a pronghorn that is slightly different from that of most other big game is the area between the eye and the base of each horn. This portion is very tight to work in, but if you proceed slowly and carefully, you should have no problems. Other than addressing these basic differences, you can proceed normally with the skinning process.

Another difference in the antelope mounting process is in the preparation of the horns. After removing the skull plate as usual, the horns and skull plate must be placed into lightly boiling water for one to two hours. The hot water prepares the horn sheath for removal from the core, and cleans the connecting membrane from the surface of the core. Without this removal, the horns will eventually begin to smell terribly, and

Antelope horns must be separated from their core so that their connective tissues can be removed.

they may also provide a haven at any time, now or in the future, for flesh-eating bugs, which can cause serious damage to the mount.

After the horn sheaths are gone and both the cores and sheaths have been thoroughly cleaned and allowed to dry, dust the interior of the sheath and the surface of the core with a small amount of dry preservative. Reattach the horn sheaths by placing a small amount of Bondo into the interior of the sheath, and then push the sheath slowly onto the horn core. Properly position it, and then set aside until each horn is fully hardened. Should any Bondo emerge from the sheath, allow it to thicken, and then use a knife to remove any excess.

With the horns cleaned and reattached, you will attach the skull plate to the manikin as usual. Then, immediately prior to pulling the skin onto the manikin and finishing the mounting process, use a small amount of black epoxy sculpt to wrap around the cores, just under the base of the antler sheath. This

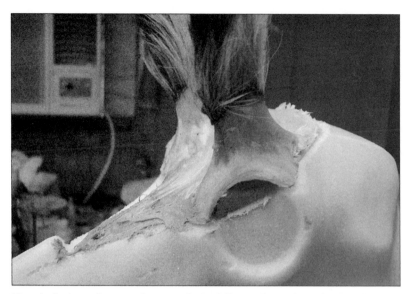

The skull plate of an antelope is a little different from that of a deer, but the procedure for attaching it is the same.

Most of the top of an antelope manikin's head is opened to make room for the skull plate.

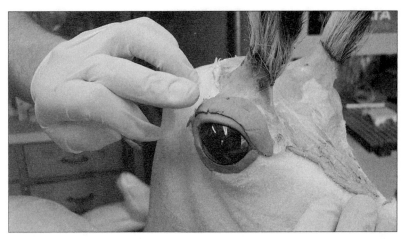

Sculpt with clay around the antelope's eyes in the same way you would for a deer.

will provide a much better transition from the skin to the horns than if the mount were to be completed with no such epoxy.

Other than these minor differences, the techniques for mounting an antelope are basically the same as for mounting a

Build up the top of the antelope's snout with sculpting clay to create a natural, smooth contour in line with the skull plate.

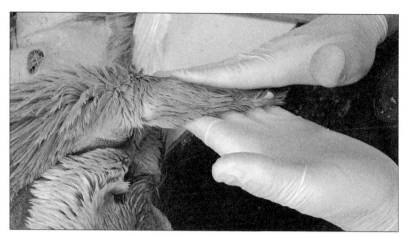

Antelope ears are pretty slim, so smooth out the Bondo inside them carefully, and take care that excess does not ooze onto the pelt.

deer. Prep the manikin, study reference, presculpt the eyes, study reference, apply adhesive, study reference, pull the skin onto the manikin, study reference—you get the picture. The photos that accompany this chapter should help in guiding you through the mounting process.

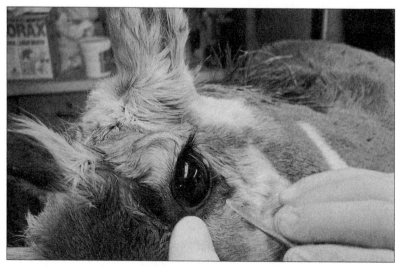

Tend carefully to the long lashes on the upper eyelids of antelope.

When you can, match the thread to the color of the pelt; use a tawny thread that conceals well in the foxy color of an antelope.

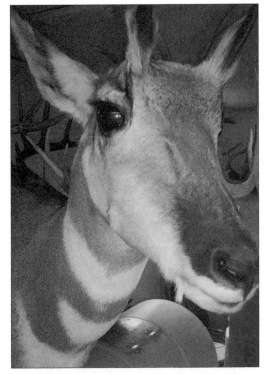

Make sure that you're able to get anatomical details of the manikin to show through on the lean face and neck of an antelope.

The smaller size of antelope make them a good candidate for an early attempt at a full-body mount.

THE AMERICAN ELK

The American elk is likely the largest project that you will ever have to deal with as a hobbyist, or even as an average professional taxidermist—at least with any frequency. Certainly, you may progress to somewhat larger animals, including African game or moose, but should that endeavor occur, it will most likely be well into the future. In addition, what you learn when mounting elk will very easily carry over to other, larger projects. Elk are ideal for large projects because they are plentiful and highly sought-after big-game animals; they take a spot on the list of the most-harvested big-game animals, just behind the pronghorn, I'd say. As I've said, white-tailed deer will make up the mainstay of all taxidermy work, followed by mule deer, black bear, antelope, and then the elk. On this list, moose, buffalo, sheep, mountain lions, and other big critters bring up the rear in total annual harvest rates. And I would surmise that in a

year's time, the number of mounts of all of these other large animals combined would be very near the total number of elk
mounts.

I have left the elk mount for our last project because it is
much larger than the deer mount, and every technique learned
so far will be used. A key difference is the fact that the applications must be stronger, along with the taxidermist's back. Elk
are basically large deer. An elk skin must be fleshed, prepped,
and tanned; the eyes, ears, nose, and lips must be turned; the
manikin must be prepped; the eyes modeled; and so on.

Note: When working with an animal the size of an elk or
larger, I recommend using a tan. Though I am a firm believer in
dry preservative, I also feel that it has its limitations when it
comes to large skins.

The necessary quantity of supplies, and thus, their cost,
will be greater with an elk. The weight of the antlers and cape
are also much greater than with a whitetail. When working
with elk ears, you'll find that they will take slightly more
Bondo when prepping and as much extra clay when building
the ear base. Other than dealing with these changes in magni-
tude, you can proceed as usual. A few more things to consider
when mounting an elk or larger big-game animal is that the
antler skull plate must be more secure and the hanger on the
back side of the manikin must be sturdier than for that of a
deer or an antelope. Also, because an elk is difficult to work
with during the initial skinning process, most capes will have a
full-length Y-incision, which means significantly more sewing
for the taxidermist.

For the project I describe here, I'll refer to a bugling elk
manikin—mouth open, nose tipped up. The elk eyes I prefer
come from the "First Honest Eye" series, from Research Mannikins.

When you order most any large manikin, the manufacturer
will most likely saw it in half to accommodate shipping—one
half being the head and a portion of the neck, the other being

the shoulders and a portion of the neck. Reassembly for this is simple. Place several tablespoons of Bondo onto the bottom section of the detached manikin, and then mix in the hardener. Spread the mixture evenly and thoroughly, and then place the top section of the manikin into place. When doing this, notice the muscle detail lines and mold lines on both the top and bottom of the manikin. These guidelines help ensure proper manikin assembly. Once both pieces are properly aligned, insert approximately ten 3- or 4-inch screws into the manikin. Angle five screws along the circumference of the manikin down toward the shoulder area, and then angle five more around the circumference of the manikin, angled toward the head. Doing this will create somewhat of a crisscross pattern and help strengthen the bond between the two halves. Allow the manikin to sit for approximately twenty minutes after reattachment is complete to allow the Bondo sufficient time to work.

Once the manikin is sturdy enough to proceed, place it onto a mounting stand, and then attach the rack. When anchor-

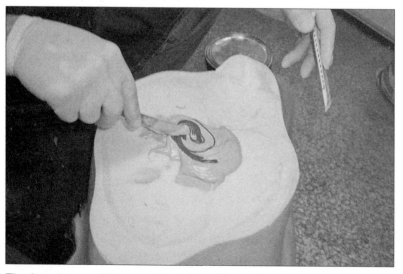

The first thing you'll have to do with an elk manikin is assemble its two big parts.

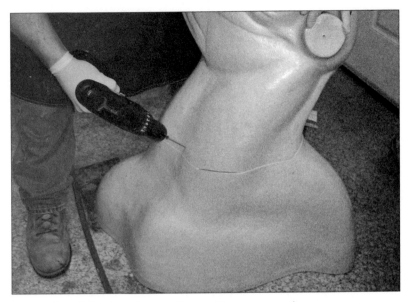

Secure the elk head to the neck base with some wood screws.

ing the skull plate of a large rack, use five or six heavy-duty, 3-inch wood screws and secure the skull plate just as you would with a deer head. Trim the skull plate as usual, and then after making certain the fit is right, place the skull plate onto a bed of Bondo that has been strengthened by excelsior that has been cut into small pieces. I prefer excelsior because it is less expensive. Depending on the size of the elk, you might need some help to set and anchor the rack onto the manikin. After seating the screws, allow the Bondo to harden, and then cover the skull plate with papier-mâché, plaster, or clay, whichever is readily available. With the antlers anchored and the skull plate sculpted, finish the preparation by roughing the manikin and cutting the tear duct slots and the lip slot.

When sculpting elk eyes, the shape that you create will be very similar to that of a deer. The main difference is that the upper brow is generally much heavier on an elk. Also, the tear

Use heavy-duty wood screws to hold the elk skull plate to the manikin; insert up to half a dozen until you're sure it is secure.

Be sure to observe the dark eyes of elk carefully to position the pupil correctly: parallel to the ground.

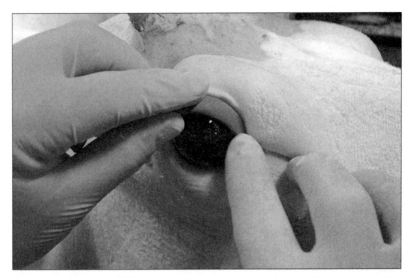

Creating elk brows follows the same procedure as for deer, except that they are heavier and require more clay.

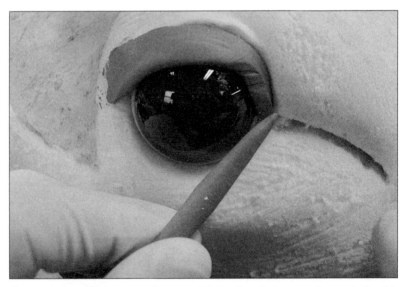

Come down a little more than an eighth of an inch over the eyeball with the top brow, and then insert the lower lid edge.

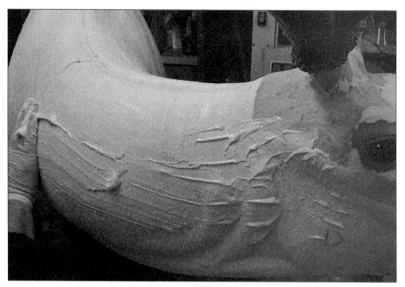

Elk have long necks and a lot of surface area, even in a shoulder mount, so apply only as much adhesive as you can work with at one time.

ducts of an elk are much larger, so to provide a smooth appearance here, apply a bit more Critter Clay both above and below each tear duct.

Now apply the adhesive, but be aware that because the incision along the back is a full-length cut, you need to leave an area ten to twelve inches wide along the back that has no adhesive. By leaving this area bare, you will alleviate any chance of adhesive getting onto the hair of the cape.

To get the cape onto the manikin, hold each side of the head and slide it to the base of the antlers, being careful not to get any adhesive on the fur, and then use a regulator needle or several long pins to anchor one side of the skin to the head. Pull the free side of the cape up along the head, lifting it to a desired position and anchoring it with nails or a regulator needle. Repeat this for the opposite side by removing the pins to allow for movement, and then position the skin and anchor it, matching the hair on either side of the seam.

Have a boxful of regulator needles ready as you prepare the mount—you'll need them to secure the cape in stages.

Because of the possibility of the skin shifting significantly during the mounting process, given the use of a full-length incision, sew the incision soon after you get the cape in place,

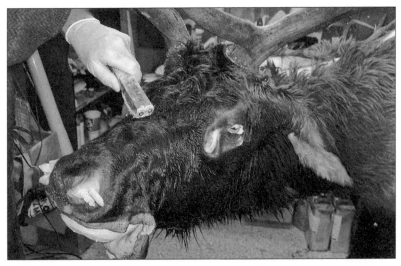

With the cape in place, smooth out some of the facial features, and then get ready to sew the incision shut along the back.

The shoulder-mount elk, just before sewing up the dorsal incision in the cape. Note the plastic bags inserted into the nostrils.

making certain that the seam is very tight; otherwise, a gap may show through once the mount is dry. Once you complete the sewing, position the skin as close as possible to the appropriate location and staple the rear of the cape to the back of the manikin. Trim the excess skin behind the manikin back, and finish the mounting process.

When completing the final modeling, pay close attention to the tear duct area. Tuck each tear duct completely, and then blend the area using the sculpting tool and a stout medium-sized paintbrush. Gradually manipulate the clay that is above and below the tear duct into place, forming a smooth transition between the exterior and interior. Pull the eyelid away from the eye area and prepare the underlying clay to accept and hold the skin attached to the eyelid. Finish sculpting the eye by modeling what you can, based on reference photos. Use the modeling tool to position the skin within the interior of each nostril, and then tuck the lips exactly as you would for a white-

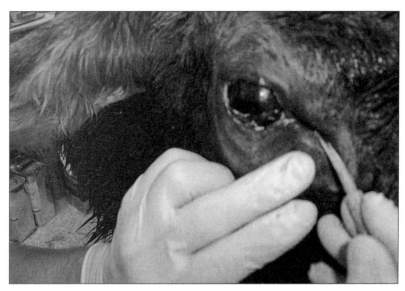

Given the size of an elk's eyes and tear ducts, they are a crucial detail that must be tended to properly for a lifelike appearance.

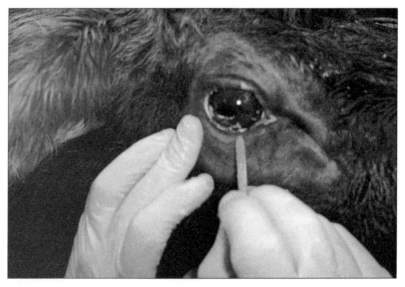

Work the clay underneath the skin around the eye to create a smooth, live-flesh look around the eye.

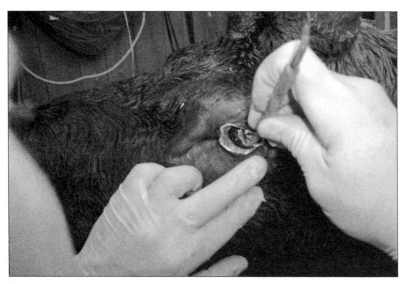

Pull the eyelid flesh out a bit and then tuck it evenly and securely into the underlying clay.

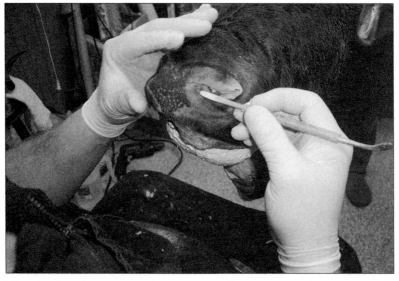

There's a lot of nose to work with on an elk, so you must be sure that you have carefully tucked it all.

tail, just compensating for their greater length or thickness with your particular elk.

An elk mount presents a lot of surface area, so check carefully along all of the elk's features to be sure that you mounted the skin correctly. Following the instructions in chapter 8 will get you through the main part of an elk mount. In chapter 11, "Perfect Finishing," you will learn how to refine those small details that are crucial to a mount and help to ensure its lifelike appearance.

CHAPTER 10

The Basics of a Full-Body Mount

A large percentage of big game taxidermists focus most of their work time on whitetails, and an even larger percentage opt for shoulder mounts for big-game animals. Some of the most common reasons for stopping short of a life-size body mount are difficulty, time, cost, and space availability. Though these reasons may be valid in many situations, creating a life-size mount is, in essence, just an extension of what you have already learned, and presents a marked increase in difficulty in only a few cases. Also, making space for at least one life-size mount is possible in most serious hunters' lives. Hey, if there's space available for the exercise bicycle/clothing hanger, certainly there is space for that once-in-a-lifetime deer, antelope, or bear.

Life-size manikins are more expensive, understandably, and rarely fit a skin perfectly, so there is significantly more sewing to do than on a shoulder mount. Other than these two major differences between a shoulder mount and a life-size mount, the basics remain the same: the essential skin and manikin preparation is addressed in the appropriate preceding chapters, and when working on a life-size mount, refer to those procedures accordingly. However, when a hunter wants to create a full-body mount, total care of the entire animal body in the field is imperative, and should be taken into consideration

No, this isn't a huge black bear, but it's a very nicely done black bear. Start with smaller individual animals for full-body mounts.

quickly. In fact, a hunter might have to make up his or her mind very quickly, sometimes, about doing a full-body mount—after a quick first inspection of the animal.

What follows are several guidelines that apply to most any life-size big game animal, whether it happens to be an antelope or a moose. By following these guidelines closely, the transition from making shoulder mounts to creating a life-size critter should be accomplished smoothly.

1. Start small. Those with little or no experience should adhere to this advice whether the mount in question is a shoulder mount, half life-size, or life-size. Though I have assisted in mounting larger life-size big game animals, the largest animals I have mounted myself without assistance have been large black bears, deer, and antelope. Reasonably speaking, very few hunters, or collectors, will ever have an elk or moose mounted life-size, but it can be done

and the finished product is beautiful—definitely a piece of wildlife art that not everyone has. Regardless of where your taxidermy interests might take you, start practicing for a full-body mount with an antelope, small deer, or small black bear. These projects can be accomplished for someone with an intermediate level of knowledge, but the beginner should get a dozen or so shoulder mounts under his or her belt before attempting one of the smaller life-size projects.

2. Always use a tanned skin when mounting a life-size mount. Though a life-size deer can be completed using dry preservative, in the hands of an experienced taxidermist, the extended length of time that will most likely be needed for completing a full mount calls for a tanned skin. Using a tanned skin will allow the taxidermist to set work aside and return as late as the following day without the detrimental side effects that most certainly would occur if using dry preservative. Remember, full-body mounts require a lot of sewing.

3. Use reference materials to help align hair patterns. Several features are apparent in a shoulder mount: The eyes, nose, and lip line are easily recognizable features that offer guidelines for the alignment of the skin on the head of most any animal. The body skin, on the other hand, is mostly free of features, or so it seems to the untrained eye. By closely studying reference, many of these unnoticeable features quickly become apparent. The trailing edge of most animal legs show a hair line where the hairs all come together to form a ridge. Many deer will be darker within a narrow strip along the center of the back. The much shorter hair of the armpit area should dictate how much skin should be tucked out of sight. The second joint from the hoof or paw should be easily discernable on all legs. And the trailing edge of the hindquarters for both deer

and antelope will offer a hair transition, from a dark hair to a relatively white hair, which should be aligned properly with opposite sides matching. These are just a few of the hair pattern alignments that are most evident, but if the burgeoning taxidermist chooses to carefully study reference photos, he or she should easily begin to find more alignment points.

4. Order life-size manikins slightly smaller than what is needed. The experienced taxidermist will order whatever manikin is closest in size and alter it to fit exact measurements. But something that a beginning taxidermist must realize is that life-size manikins rarely, and possibly never, fit exactly. To get this exact fit, a manikin must be purchased and then altered for this extent of exactness. For the beginning to intermediate taxidermists, this type of advanced manikin alteration will come later. At this earlier stage of experience, take the best measurements possible, and then order a manikin very close to those measurements, but one that is ever so slightly on the small size. Doing so will alleviate any problems that may be encountered with a manikin that is too large.

5. Use plenty of quality adhesive. Just as with a shoulder mount, a quality adhesive will allow the taxidermist to move the skin into position after it has been pulled onto the manikin and completely sewn. Using an ample amount of quality adhesive will also alleviate any drumming that may occur during the drying period. The best method to apply this adhesive is progressively, using a small amount on a small area at a time, until the skin has been pulled fully onto the manikin. Doing so will help prevent excessive amounts of adhesive getting onto the hair.

6. Make certain that the seam is unnoticeable. Many taxidermists often make much longer stitches when mounting a life-size mount, probably due to having to do much more

sewing than on a shoulder mount. However, don't let a lengthy sewing job negatively affect a quality-finished product. Making stitches that are tight and closely spaced will ensure that the finished mount has no portions of the seam that show through the hair or through hair patterns that shift significantly.

7. Gather as much experience as possible before attempting this project. Mount several deer and possibly other big game shoulder mounts. Then talk with other taxidermists to gather as much information as possible. A good source of information about full-body mounts might be found in a local taxidermist association. Then, once all this is complete, a life-size mount should be attainable, without going completely nuts. In addition, the last major need to ensure a quality life-size mount is, you guessed it, reference, reference, and more reference.

CHAPTER 11

Perfect Finishing

With the mounting procedure complete, put the mount aside for a short time before continuing. This will allow everything to dry properly. After drying, any shrinkage that takes place will be minimal and the paints and epoxies applied afterward will adhere much better. The type of animal, humidity, temperature, and preservation method all dictate the amount of time that should be allotted for proper drying.

Some taxidermists use a drying room, which is basically an airtight room that contains a dehumidifier and a large fan. Using such a room should produce a completely dry mount within five to ten days. Unassisted drying will take much longer, possibly up to three weeks, depending on the environment. The beginner does best to let the mount sit in a room that is suitable for comfortable living; 60 to 80 degrees Fahrenheit with humidity from 20 to 60 percent is ideal. Since I live in the South, I often have trouble finding humidity below 80 percent during spring and summer, but at 70 degrees, most mounts will dry with no problem, even in an area of elevated humidity.

To check for the proper drying of a mount, insert a finger into the ear. The ear butt or clay placed there is usually the last area to dry, so if this area is dry, the mount should be dry enough to continue working. To be on the safe side, if no drying room is available, allow at least three weeks before doing any finish work to the mount. Then, as you gain experience, you may be able to adjust your minimal drying times a bit.

Once a mount has dried, you will notice that much of the skin's natural color around the eyes, on the nose, and within the ears has been lost. You must replace those colors to duplicate the live animal. Also, as a mount dries, shrinkage will occur in all areas, but especially to those areas that haven't been fleshed properly. You must rebuild any areas where shrinkage may have occurred. As mentioned, proper fleshing will minimize shrinkage, so if the mount shrinks considerably you will know to be more attentive to the fleshing requirements on the next mount. If shrinkage is minimal, you have done a good job. The only additional area to finish with epoxy would be on a mount with an open mouth. The lip line will have to be blended into the jawset, and for some animals the teeth will have to be stained and the inner lip painted to simulate a lifelike appearance. This occurs primarily with bears, but when mounting an open-mouth elk or deer, these requirements will also hold true.

For the finish work you will need paints, an airbrush, epoxies, and paintbrushes for blending the epoxies. The paints are for replacing any colors while the epoxies will be used to rebuild any shrunken areas. Several brands of paint and epoxy are available and can be purchased from Research Mannikins. Though some veteran taxidermists insist on oil paints that are brushed on as well as wax for rebuilding shrunken areas, many others in our field, including myself, prefer an airbrush loaded with a paint specifically formulated for taxidermy. Also, two-part epoxies seem to adhere to the mount and hold paint much better than other, more primitive alternatives.

Most paint manufacturers offer mammal paint kits. These kits usually contain every color needed for general big-game finishing. During the learning stages these basic paints should be suitable. Then, as experience builds, you will probably begin to find additional colors which aid in bringing a mount to life. Taxidermy-specific paints can be purchased in either water- or lacquer-base. I don't recommend applying the two on the same mount. In other words, don't use one coat of a water-based paint and then spray a lacquer over the top, as this will cause problems. Choose one type of paint and then stick with it. Which one is right for you? Well, only you can decide. I personally use lacquers, but this is due largely to the way I was taught. After doing a bit of research I would like to give water-based paints a try, but as I already own an abundance of lacquer-based paints, I am hesitant to change. Both types have advantages and disadvantages.

A major advantage of a lacquer-based paint is that it dries much more quickly than a water-based paint. Most times, a lacquer will dry almost as soon as you apply it. The disadvantage of lacquer-based paints is the health risk that they pose—their fumes can be toxic—and they are also highly flammable. Whenever you use any paint, you should wear a respirator, but when using lacquers, a respirator is mandatory. Also, when using lacquers, proper ventilation of the work space is a must, as this cuts down on the buildup of fumes.

The obvious advantages of a water-based paint include the fact that they are not as harmful to a user's health and they are not flammable. You can get away with not using a respirator while using water-based paints. In addition, you can thin water-based paint with, of course, water, which is very convenient, or with acetone, which will produce a quicker drying time than plain water. The only major disadvantage with water-based paint is the slower drying time.

In addition to the necessary paints, you'll need an epoxy to deal with shrinkage. Most two-part epoxies are very similar. They consist of two substances that are a bit stiffer than clay. Mix the two parts together thoroughly in a fifty-fifty ratio to activate the epoxy and stimulate hardening. After mixing, most epoxies will provide an hour or more of working time before becoming too hard to work with. Another popular material for rebuilding shrunken areas is epoxy clay. It differs from regular epoxy in that it is clay-based, but offers some of the same attributes of a regular epoxy. Epoxy clay consists of two parts that must be mixed thoroughly together after which hardening takes place within a couple of hours. It will texture slightly better than regular epoxies, and paint will adhere very well to this substance.

ESSENTIAL STEPS FOR FINISHING A MOUNT

No matter the species, finishing a mount moves through the same stages, with the exception of the color scheme that may change slightly from one animal to another. For open-mouth mounts, obviously, the interior of the mouth between the jawset and the lip skin will have to be filled with epoxy and properly finished. (See below for further information on finishing open-mouth mounts.)

Cleaning the Surfaces

Before finishing any mount, take a small wire brush to the eye, nose, and inner ear areas and brush away any loose particles or underlying epidermis that may remain loosely attached to the skin's surface. Be careful around the glass eyes, because most scratch easily, especially synthetic or hard-plastic versions. Continue by brushing the entire mount thoroughly with a grooming brush, similar to one that would be used for dog grooming. Then use compressed air to blow off the entire mount. Doing this will help to rid the mount of any loose hair or skin. Cleaning of the aforementioned surfaces is very important, because if you were to paint over the top of any loose skin or other substance, it could later become detached and

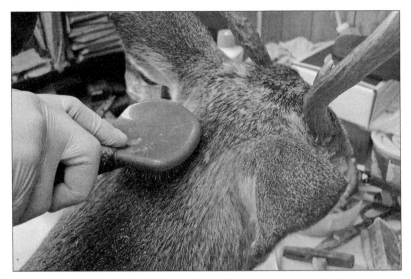

Gently groom all the fur on the mount with a short-bristle brush to neaten its appearance.

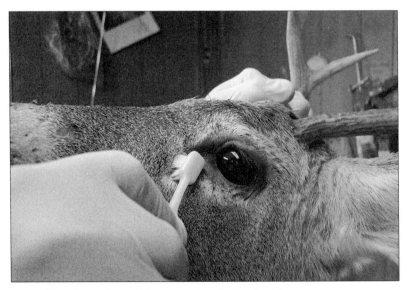

A toothbrush works well for arranging the fur in tight spots.

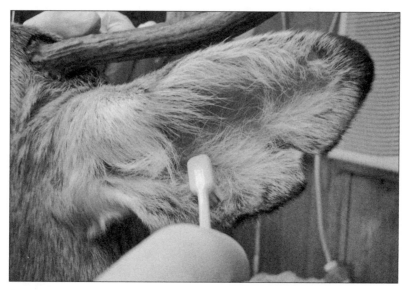

Clean the ear hair of debris, but don't make it look perfect, as if it were "combed."

create a bare spot that would show through the finish. To avoid this problem, properly and thoroughly clean the eye, nose, and ear areas.

Rebuilding with Epoxy

After you clean the mount, continue using the two-part epoxy to rebuild any shrunken areas. Carefully examine the skin portion of each eyelid adjacent to the eyelashes. During the mounting process, the eyelid will lay against the eye, but as drying takes place this skin will pull away a fraction. How much shrinkage occurs again depends on the thoroughness of the fleshing. If you performed the fleshing process properly, the gap between eye and eyelid after drying will probably be less than a sixteenth of an inch. But on a poorly fleshed cape, this gap may widen to more than an eighth of an inch. Use epoxy to fill in this gap. Using a sculpting tool, place a small

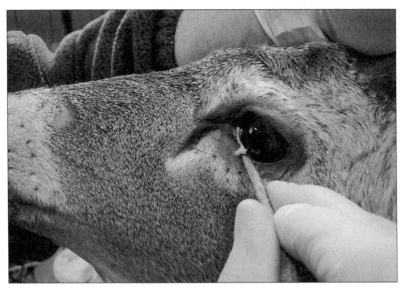

Use epoxy to fill in the gaps where the skin might pull away from the eyes.

Push the epoxy into small gaps with the sculpting tool, filling in even the smallest cracks due to drying.

amount of epoxy between the eye and eyelid. Do this with the flat end of a sculpting tool to force the filler into this small crevice. Continue this process around the eye.

Once you move near the front and rear areas of the eye, you might encounter damaged areas due to the fleshing process. If so, now is the time to rebuild these areas, thus simulating the eye of a live animal. Once you fill in or repair all the areas around the eyes, remove any excess epoxy with the sculpting tool, and then use a thick paintbrush dipped in lacquer thinner to smooth and blend the applied epoxies to the skin of the eyelid. If done properly, the junction of epoxy and skin will not be detectable to the human eye.

The interior of each nostril is another key area that will require the application of an epoxy. Using the sculpting tool, insert small amounts of epoxy into each nostril. Then begin to shape the interior of each nostril, matching that of your reference photos. When shaping the nostrils, dip the end of the

Remove any plastic fillers from the nostrils, then take a look at the interiors and smooth them with epoxy where need be.

sculpting tool into lacquer thinner or water, which will help the epoxy to shape easily and smoothly, avoiding any rough edges that may occur otherwise.

Closed-Mouth Mounts

One last prominent feature that might require rebuilding is the lower lip. Most big-game animals will show the bottom lip when the mouth is closed, though not always. To combat shrinkage during the drying process, you should rebuild this lip area slightly to simulate a fleshy appearance. Offering a finished product with a fleshy lower lip will definitely add that little something that increases a mount's lifelike look.

To rebuild the lower lip, roll a pea-sized portion of epoxy between your fingers, forming a rounded length. Apply this to the lower lip area and use the sculpting tool to gradually begin blending and smoothing the epoxy. Don't overdo this application because you want the added epoxy to flow naturally from the skin. Your best approach is to form this section of lip slightly too small rather than at what seems to be the actual size. Then after forming the general shape of the lip line, use the paintbrush to smooth and blend the epoxy to the skin. This should complete the rebuilding process of a mount that has a closed mouth.

Open-Mouth Mounts

Open-mouth mounts are very popular with nearly all predator species and sometimes with elk and the odd flehming deer. This type of pose definitely adds excitement to any game room or trophy collection. As a taxidermist I have seen plenty of interior mouth work over the years, and I can tell you that good mouth work always adds a lot to any mount. On the other hand, poor mouth work greatly detracts from an otherwise good mount. On some of the worst mounts I've seen, the taxidermist didn't even attempt to fill in the gap between the skin and jawset—a flaw that is evident even to most eight-year-olds.

Jawsets

Taxidermists complete the majority of their open-mouth mounts with a plastic, acrylic, or wax jawset that sits conveniently in the open mouth of the manikin. You will usually install a jawset before beginning the mounting process, but if possible, you can choose to install the jawset after the drying process is complete. Installing the jawset after the mount is complete and dry can provide the taxidermist more room to work within the mouth during the mounting process. This is due to the fact that without the jawset in place the mouth area is actually a large hole or void, as no teeth, gums, or tongue are in place. This facilitates much easier tucking of the lip skin. But frequently, you will have to install the jawset prior to the mounting process because it will not fit into the mouth of the manikin after assembly is complete. This is dependent on the manufacturer of the manikin and the particular jawset being used. If you choose to install the jawset after mounting, you must test-fit it to make certain it will fit into the open mouth of the manikin before you begin mounting.

With most open-mouth manikins, the top of the head comes off, making jaw-fitting very easy. Additionally, both the top and bottom sections of the mouth on open-mouth manikins are designed to accept most jawsets readily, with very little or no modification. Note that the mouth area on some manikins is filled with foam that must be cut or Dremeled away. This is inconvenient, but in some situations such manikins are the only ones available for a particular size or pose.

To install the jawset into a manikin with a removable head piece, first remove the top section of the head. Next, ensure the proper fit of the lower jaw into the bottom portion of the manikin. Most open-mouth manikins carry instructions that suggest a corresponding jawset. If you follow this recommendation, the jawset should fit, with no alterations necessary. But if not, you might have to make some slight modifications. Presuming a good fit, continue by mixing a small portion of Bondo and spread it onto the inner bottom area of the lower section of the jawset, and also apply a small amount to the bottom jaw of the jawset. Attach the two pieces in place in the mouth, positioning them correctly, and then hold both until the Bondo begins to solidify. Repeat this procedure for the top jaw, setting the pieces into the section that you removed from the manikin's head. Then rejoin this top portion of the head with the top jaw attached to the head of the manikin. Do this by placing a small amount of Bondo where the top portion makes contact on the head, and then press together and align. Hold the upper jaw and head portion in place until the Bondo begins to harden. This will complete the installation of the jawset.

To strengthen the jawset installation and the head junction, scratch the smooth surface using the Stout Ruffer or other roughing tool of the manikin in any area where Bondo is to be applied. Using a sculpting tool, dig out a couple shallow chunks in the center of the attachment area, as this will also improve strength. In addition, a 3-inch screw can be inserted through the top of the head of the manikin. At this point the screw should be tightened thoroughly prior to the hardening of the Bondo.

Mouth Inserts or Cups

In addition to conventional jawsets, which require more finishing work, advances in the taxidermy industry have created various *mouth inserts* or *cups*. Mouth cups are presculpted inserts that have a fleshy and accurate lip line, along with highly detailed mouth interiors, including the back of the throat. Some jawsets come out of the box prefinished, which means all the taxidermist has to do is simply blend the mouth insert to the skin junction. Instead of applying epoxy to form the gum and interior lip, you'll use very small portions of epoxy to join the preserved skin to the lip line. These mouth cups are available for bear as well as flehming deer and bugling elk.

Installing and accurately attaching a mouth cup is relatively easy. You'll make this joint initially during the mounting process. The junction along the lip line where the haired area and the hair-free area meet is where the skin joins the insert. Instead of attaching to the hairless lip skin, as usual, carefully cut the lip line along the hair line before the mounting process. Removal of this unwanted skin is very easy. Using your scalpel, cut the skin one or two millimeters into the hairless side of the line formed by the hair and hairless junction in the lip area. Make this cut entirely around the mouth. Then during the mounting process, make sure that any hair patterns, such as at the rear corners of the mouth or each side of the nose pad, line up before permanently joining the skin to the insert. These hair patterns are generally most evident at the rear corners of the mouth and in the center of the chin and nose. Make certain that the joint area between the skin and the artificial mouth cup is very tight, ensuring that no gaps will occur. As drying takes place, the skin may pull slightly from the insert. You can fill this gap with epoxy, but your goal is to keep this separation minimal. To lock the skin tightly to the insert, use a five-minute epoxy, which is an adhesive epoxy in liquid form, along the outer half-inch of the jaw area during the mounting process. This will serve to lock the skin down tightly before any drying takes place. Use your sculpting tool or butter knife to spread a thin layer of this epoxy along the skin area adjacent to the presculpted lip area. Be careful when using a five-minute epoxy, however, because if you're not, you could make a terrible, possibly irreparable mistake.

After the mount is completely dry, finishing the skin and mouth-insert junction can be relatively simple if you have properly completed the mounting process. To finish this connection, use the same two-part epoxy that you used for the eyelid edges and inner nostril areas. These two-part epoxies come in several different colors. For most big game I recommend using pink. Though some skin tones may be dark in appearance, they will generally have underlying pinkish skin tones.

After choosing a color, mix the two parts into a small amount, approximately the size of a marble, then take the small portion and form it into the shape of a pencil. Pinch off a small portion and continue to roll it between your hands, making it longer but with a much smaller diameter. When the diameter seems appropriately sized—about half the size of a pencil—begin to lay the epoxy into the crevice located at the line formed by the junction of the mouth cup and the skin. As you place the epoxy into the small crevice, begin to blend it into the artificial lip line as well as the skin. However, if the insert is prepainted, dip the sculpting tool in water rather than lacquer thinner to avoid removing any paint along the lip line of the mouth insert.

Completely fill in all gaps along this skin-mouth cup junction, and then proceed to further blend it using a paintbrush dipped in water (again, avoiding any paint removal that may occur by using a lacquer thinner). Further blending can be completed using 100-grit sandpaper prior to the final hardening of the epoxy. Dampen the sandpaper with water and lightly *press* the joined area, as this will give the epoxy a textured finish rather than an unaltered slick appearance. After the epoxy junction is fully blended, a small amount of paint might be needed to further blend any opposing colors. When applying the necessary paint, apply a very small amount, and then continue lightly adding paint until you create a smooth color flow.

Most suppliers that sell mouth cups also offer specific manikin forms that they have sculpted to match. This generally aids in assembly. Otherwise, you might have to perform extensive alterations of a manikin, and with little or no experience in manikin alteration, you might have a difficult time. So if you choose to use a mouth insert, make certain that you can find a manikin designed to accept that insert. If not, you will probably do best to use a conventional two-piece jawset.

Artificial Noses

I suggest learning to mount a nose conventionally first, but once you have accomplished this, another great technique to master is the use of an artificial nose. Artificial noses are a nice choice because the inner detail of each nostril is already sculpted. Also, the outer surface is fleshy and highly detailed to match that of a live animal.

Using an artificial nose is very simple, and some mouth inserts have an artificial nose already attached. If not, you can easily attach an artificial nose by cutting out an appropriate attachment point on the manikin and applying a small amount of five-minute epoxy. After attaching the nose to the manikin, mounting and finishing procedures are identical to those used when securing the skin to a jaw insert. If you are careful to use the appropriate size and line up any hair patterns, the procedure should go smoothly.

Artificial noses also serve as excellent three-dimensional references for those who want to work with the actual nose of the animal.

Finish Painting

For many big-game animals such as elk, buffalo, bear, and antelope, dark brown can be used for the majority of the necessary finish painting. This includes the areas around the eyes and the nose. The nose will probably offer the most variation from one animal to another. The nose may appear black, but if you look very closely, the color is probably more of a dark brown. Applying a black color to the nose will only tend to create a harsh, unnatural appearance. Other frequently used colors include: a cream color or buckskin tan, offered by several taxidermy paint suppliers for the inner ears of deer, elk, and moose; a rich brown, which will serve to blend darker to lighter colors around the eyes and tear ducts; and off-white mixed with dusty pink to give the appearance of a light fleshy area to the interior of the nostrils. For open-mouth mounts, the list of colors needed will extend to those offered primarily for jawset detailing, such Mohr Flesh, which will provide a purple-pinkish color that simulates the gum area of most animals.

Because this book is intended to cover the basics of a broad subject, and because there is a wide assortment of big-game animals that you may encounter while practicing taxidermy, the learning taxidermist should try to obtain individual color schedules that cover in detail the required paints and application procedures on a species-by-species basis. These are generally available at no charge from quality taxidermy suppliers. After completing several big-game mounts, most taxidermists tend to develop a personal paint schedule that suits their individual needs.

Applying a Sealer

To continue with the finishing process, after a proper cleaning and the application of epoxies is completed, apply a base coat of sealer to all the skin areas that need to be painted. This will help any additional layers of paint to adhere to the mount. Apply two to three light layers rather than one thick layer. This base-coat sealer should be applied to the area surrounding the eye, the interior of the ears, and the nose pad, and, if necessary, to the interior of an open mouth. Once the sealer has been applied and has dried, continue to add color according to your reference materials or paint schedules. For these final paint applications, live reference along with plenty of practice with an airbrush and various paints are very beneficial.

Keep in mind that the taxidermist's primary goal is to make the mount look natural, not painted. So be very sparing with any paint applied. During the learning stages you should stop short of what appears to be enough paint. This will prevent overpainting.

After all the paints have dried, you must apply a sealant. This will help seal the paint and avoid paint loss. Apply base-coat sealer around the eyes. Then apply a satin to the eyelid itself, but do so sparingly. Your goal is to create a semiwet eyelid, but an eye that has been glossed will appear unnatural. Consulting your reference photos helps, but observation of live animals is crucial to re-creating the kind of sheen that's found around a live eye.

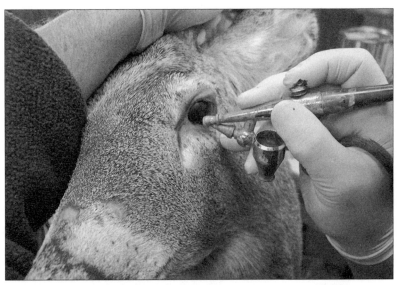

Go very lightly when trying to create the wet sheen on an animal's eye. A glossy eye will appear unnatural.

Continue by spraying the interior of the ear with satin, as this should produce the waxy appearance commonly found in most animals' ears. Once you've finished all the touch-ups, you'll need to apply a coat of gloss to the nose. This is the only area where I use a gloss. As mentioned previously, some taxidermists insist upon using a gloss around the eyes and within the interior of the ears, but in my opinion, this appears cartoon-like. Sometimes the nose can appear dry under natural circumstances. You can quickly find a reference for this by looking at a dog's nose, which sometimes has a dry appearance, while other times will appear quite glossy from moisture. If you prefer a dry appearance on the nose, apply a satin or a base-coat sealer atop the applied colors. A satin color will offer a semi-dry appearance whereas a base-coat sealer will provide a very dry appearance. With all the top coats applied, the finishing should be complete.

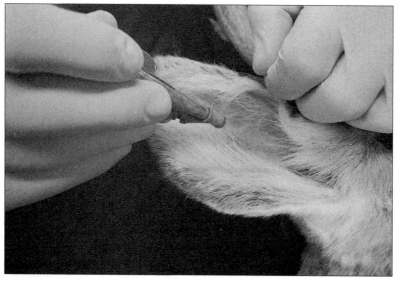

Lightly spray a clear satin into the deer's ear to create a naturally waxy surface.

How wet-looking you make a deer's nose is your call, but a dry-looking nose is not unnatural.

Without a doubt, the finishing process is vital to the accuracy of any mount. If the opportunity presents itself, look closely at mounted animals of all kinds. Some taxidermists will even go so far as to add what appears to be dew on the whiskers, simulating the condensation that occurs when animals are breathing in cold air. Other additions that I have noticed include dimples on the nose pad, along with a fleshy underlying base color. All of these small extras add to the realism of any mount, and without a doubt, this finishing work can make or break the realistic effect that we all strive to achieve through the taxidermy process. Onlookers with no experience or understanding of the taxidermy process will most likely not key in on an armpit or throat patch that is shifted slightly, or notice poorly set eyes, but they will definitely notice a harsh color on the eyes, nose, or ears. They will also notice if over-spray has misted onto surrounding hair or if they see uneven epoxy within the tear ducts or nostrils.

When you look at a finished mount and it seems like it might move, you know you've done your job right.

Clearly, the perfection of your mount is solidified by proper finishing. The better you get at the basics, the more time you can dedicate to finishing. But no matter how much experience you gain, tweaking and perfecting your finishing techniques is a never-ending process. You'll always be searching for that incredible detail—condensation on the whiskers, or hairs on the tongue—that takes the notion of "lifelike" to new levels.

CHAPTER 12

Plaques and European Mounts

The mounting process certainly makes up the bulk of taxidermy, but there are other projects that can enhance our pleasure afield, as well as provide the satisfaction of completing a worthwhile project—with very little time and cost, comparatively speaking. A couple of taxidermists' favorites for many years have been the antler plaque and the European mount. Both provide a trophy that is enjoyable, and offer something a little different for the hunter who may already have an abundance of mounts.

ANTLER PLAQUES

In the past, some hunters have simply cut the antlers from their trophy and nailed them to the side of a barn or their house, but after several years' exposure, this method of display causes sun damage to the antlers, thus reducing the aesthetic appeal of what was once a valuable prize for the hunter. The obvious thing to do is to place the antlers onto a plaque, finish the exterior (or provide a cover for the skull plate), and place the rack inside the home.

The steps required to finish a plaque are rather simple, but for a quality finished appearance, you must do a bit more work beyond simply getting a plaque kit from the local sporting goods store and throwing it together.

You've got two possible approaches: either use a commercial cover to place over the cleaned skull plate, attaching both to a hardwood or laminated panel; or, cover the skull plate using papier-mâché and leather, and then attach it to a hardwood panel. I suggest using a solid hardwood panel when custom-covering a skull plate, because it adds a high-quality appearance to the custom product.

To use a commercial cover, simply order a desired plaque cover, and then carefully trim the skull plate to fit the chosen panel. Once the skull plate sits on the panel in a way that creates an appealing angle of the antlers, attach the skull plate to the panel using four or more wood screws of an appropriate length. Next, trim the cover to fit across the skull plate and around each antler base. Also, make certain that the cover will fit flush to the panel. This is rather simple, but it's important to ensure that the antlers are attached firmly to the panel, and that

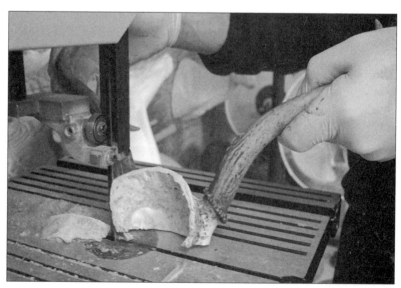

A jigsaw is the easiest way to trim a skull plate, but you can do so by hand.

no scratches or dents are applied to the panel. To strengthen the skull plate once it has been trimmed, fill the interior void of the skull plate with Bondo, and then shape accordingly to allow the skull plate to sit flat against the panel.

Building a custom panel can offer a custom appearance and will provide the owner with a product that is unique compared to other commercially made panels. Also, when building a custom panel, the skull-plate base can be customized to a desirable shape and color, or with a covering of whatever material you most prefer.

To get started on a custom panel, trim the skull plate to an appropriate shape and an acceptable angle. Then, trim a thin portion of plywood that will be attached to the base of the skull plate, in order to facilitate easy attachment to a panel. The shape of this plywood is usually similar to a water droplet, with the point of the droplet facing downward when attached to the base of the skull plate. Position the skull plate on the plywood

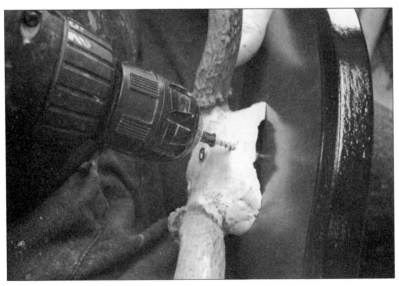

Be careful to drill precisely when working with a stained and finished plaque—you won't get many chances to mess up.

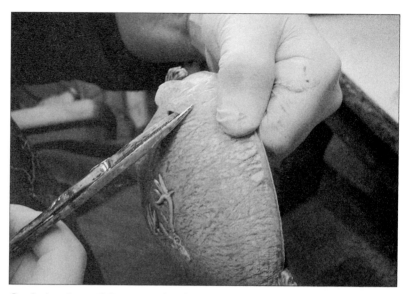

Cut holes that will fit pretty closely to the diameter of the antlers.

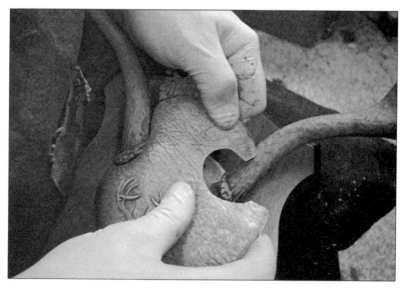

You can use Bondo to build up the skull plate and create a more rounded, flush fit with the leather cover.

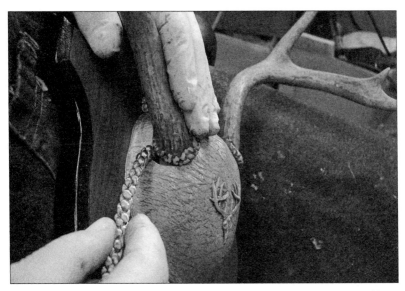

Some kits come with braids that wrap each antler base to make for a flush fit. Or, you can create such braids yourself out of rawhide.

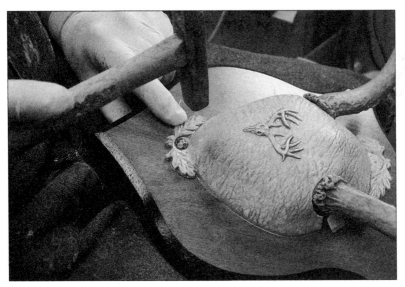

Secure the cover with the nails provided. Clear sealer can be used to close the gaps behind the antlers.

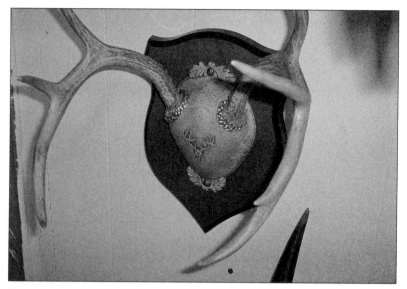

Such a mount might be a lot less expensive than a full shoulder mount, but it's still pretty classy.

backing, and place marks around the edge of the plywood. Then, fill the base of the skull plate with Bondo and press the plywood into position, lining up the marks that you made.

Once the Bondo has hardened, flip the rack over, allowing the attached plywood backing to sit flat to the floor. Now use papier-mâché to fill any voids between the skull plate and the backboard, and create a shape around and atop the skull plate until an even, rounded appearance is achieved. After the papier-mâché has dried thoroughly, cover the skull plate with leather, using wood glue as an adhesive. Take your time attaching the leather, making sure you glue it evenly. To secure the leather to the skull base, wrap it to the back side where the plywood is located and secure it with staples.

Once the leather has dried, locate four points on the plate where you can create small pilot holes for the sake of inserting screws to secure the antler plate to a hardwood panel. Quality

You don't need good wood for the base, just a proper-sized piece of plywood. Note the Bondo-filled skull plate.

Secure the plywood base to the skull plate with four to five wood screws, the heavier the better for large antlers.

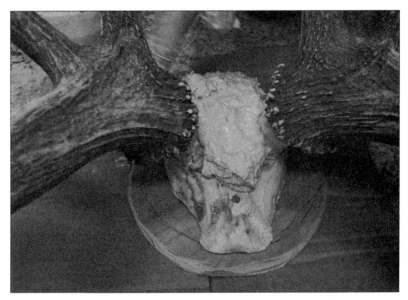

Trim the plywood base so it fits more closely the shape of the skull plate.

Fill in any spaces around the skull plate and base with papier-mâché until you create a uniform shape.

Cover the form with wood glue, in preparation for wrapping.

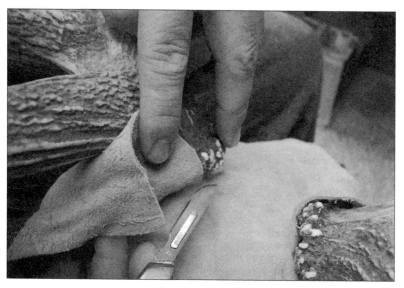

Wrap the form with leather, being careful to keep the leather even, and cut tightly around the bases of the antlers.

Secure the leather on the back of the base with a staple gun.

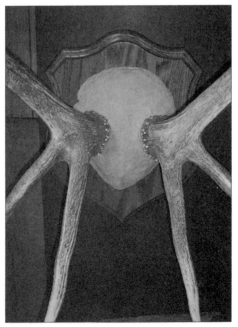

When you've got some nice antlers, nothing that's "once-in-a-lifetime," or you need to save space, the antler mount is the way to go.

brass-head wood screws are what you want—something that goes with the look of the leather. These screws should be long enough to penetrate the skull plate and the plywood, and further bite into the plaque.

EUROPEAN MOUNTS

This name may be deceiving, because technically speaking, a "European mount" isn't a mount at all. This type of mount is actually the cleaned and whitened skull of most any trophy, including antlered game such as deer, elk, and moose, or predators such as bear or mountain lion.

To begin the preparation of a European mount, remove the skull from the carcass and use a knife or scalpel to remove as much flesh from it as possible. This should include the removal of the eyes as well as the tongue, and taxidermists usually also remove the lower jaw of an antlered animal. Removing as much tissue as possible is certainly helpful, but it isn't mandatory, as the bulk of flesh removal will occur later.

You can choose one of several methods for thorough flesh removal: boiling, the use of dermestid beetles, or soaking the skull in fresh water for several weeks. All methods have drawbacks as well as benefits, but boiling is probably the most convenient for the average person. (Using beetles to clean skulls is ideal, but this can be expensive if the skulls must be sent to a third party. And since the average taxidermist does not generally produce enough European-mount work to sustain a colony of beetles, owning a colony isn't wise, or easy.)

Occasionally, I allow the skull to sit in plain water for several weeks, and then replace with fresh water and allow the skull to sit for several more weeks. This process actually works exceptionally well, especially in the summer months, but the smell is horrible. For that reason, the pot must be located some distance from any home, or there will be plenty of complaints from either the spouse or the neighbors.

Boiling, therefore, is probably the easiest way to go. Although some taxidermists insist that boiling weakens and slightly shrinks the skull, unless the skull being cleaned and bleached is that of a bear or a mountain lion that just meets the barest minimum requirements for the record books, any detrimental effects of boiling will be nearly indiscernible, even to those who are knowledgeable about the process.

The equipment required to boil most any skull is a large pot and a heat source. Many years ago, I would sometimes use a Coleman camp stove, but since then I have moved on to a bet-

The basic outdoor cooker setup: pot, cooking stand, and propane tank.

ter cooking system, utilizing a propane cooking stand similar to the type used for deep frying or outdoor cooking. These can be found at a relatively low cost at most sporting goods stores or marts and they work exceptionally well for these projects, even doubling as an outdoor cooker (as long as you're sure to use a different pot for this).

To get started, place the skulls into the pot and fill it with water. Boiling water that covers the lower section of the antlers typically does not have a detrimental effect. The only problem might come from fat within the skull that will thin and float to the top upon boiling, where it tends to gather around and cling to the portion of antler that is submersed. To combat this, wrap the base of each antler tightly with aluminum foil before the immersion. This will usually prevent the fat from clinging to the antler. After the boiling process is complete, remove the aluminum foil along with any contaminants.

With the skulls placed into the cooking pot, turn the burner to a low setting. The goal here is to reach a heat just under the true boiling point, creating a very light boil. Some taxidermists add *sal soda* or *washing soda* (sodium carbonate), which aids in the removal of the flesh. Sal soda is available through most taxidermy suppliers. Other taxidermists have told me that they have substituted a clothing detergent to aid in flesh removal, and they have reported that this worked equally as well as sal soda.

Continue the boiling process for an hour or more, and then remove and allow the skull to cool. After cooling, remove as much tissue as possible. Use a knife to cut or scrape away any stubborn flesh. When as much flesh as possible has been removed, put the skull back into the boiling pot, top off the water, and repeat the boiling process. Do this as many times as necessary to remove all of the flesh. Be careful when working with the skull during the boiling process, as well as afterwards, because the teeth will become loose and some may be lost from the skull. To prevent this, inspect the skull each time it is handled, and if a tooth is found to be missing, strain the contents from the boiling pot or pour the water onto a surface where the tooth can be easily found. Having all necessary teeth intact is important to the appearance of a European mount.

Once the skull is completely cleaned, leave it in the sun to dry thoroughly. Then inspect the teeth for any that might be loose. If any loose teeth are found, glue them into place using a Super Glue gel.

There are several different whitening agents available for whitening the skull. However, it's important that you never use Clorox bleach, as it will continue to break down the skull even after the process is complete, eventually making the skull chalky and more fragile. Whitening is best completed with a twenty- to forty-volume peroxide, which can be purchased in bulk at most beauty supply stores. Peroxide, along with a powdered whitening additive, can also be purchased in small amounts from many taxidermy suppliers.

I prefer to use forty-volume peroxide in a cream base. The cream base is very thick and can be brushed onto the skull, where it will generally stay long enough to complete the task of whitening. To get the most from this type of whitening, use a clear plastic bag large enough to accommodate the skull, and then brush the cream-based peroxide onto the skull, wrap the bag tightly closed, and place the skull in the sun. The heat and the sunshine seem to enhance the effects of the peroxide. Be very careful when using any peroxide—wear protective gear, including rubber gloves, goggles, and an apron. Also, avoid getting any peroxide onto the antlers or any other surrounding materials, because doing so will severely whiten the surface, and it might cause excessive damage.

Once the skull is whitened completely, you can simply display it as is—setting it on a shelf or a mantel, or you can attach it to a panel.

Attachment to a panel is rather simple. You can drill two to three appropriately positioned holes into the panel then use

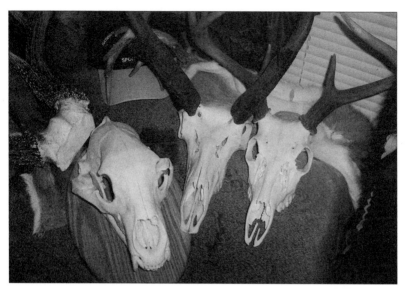

A European mount can go anywhere—let it sit up on a bookshelf or mantle, or attach it to a plaque for wall hanging, like the bear skull at left.

wood screws of an appropriate length to secure the skull to the panel. To strengthen the skull it is best to place a couple tablespoons of Bondo into the rear portion of the nasal cavity, and possibly into the brain cavity. This will give the screws a solid substance to take hold of, rather than the bone material alone.

CHAPTER 13

Tips for Making Mounts Come to Life

Throughout my years as a taxidermist I have learned many hard lessons. Some, after the fact, were obvious, while others were not.

What follows here are some of the most beneficial lessons I have learned, which should help the beginner avoid some time-consuming and often costly mistakes. There are other obstacles that you will encounter along the way, but the issues discussed below are those that became significant to me.

Lessons Learned

1. It's important to choose the correct manikin.

This seems like an elementary step, but many beginners (and even some trained taxidermists) will insist on using a form that is too large for the skin. The human thought process seems to dictate that bigger is better. In taxidermy, this is far from the truth. Most times, a larger-than-accurate manikin will only present problems.

A second manikin-choice problem that I quickly ran into was choosing a pose with no regard to the measurements taken from the skin and carcass. Very early in my taxidermy career I had taken my first bobcat, and without hesitation I decided to mount it. Although I had spent considerable hours skinning, sewing, and otherwise helping with various mounting processes at my father's shop, I had never been responsible—or knowledgeable—enough to complete the entire procedure on my own. So the first thing I did was pick up a taxidermy supply catalog and choose a pose for my bobcat. Size didn't matter to me at that point, because all bobcats are the same size . . . right?

Once I'd received the manikin shipment, I continued with the mounting process. After several hours of stretching and pulling, sweating and cursing—as well as cutting and whittling away at the manikin—I decided it would have been much easier to have started with a manikin of the correct size. From then on I took very accurate measurements of all animals that were to be mounted. This crucial lesson has never left my mind.

2. Use your imagination to deal with damaged areas.

If a skin suffers damage, all is not lost. As I've said, the level of field care often determines the best possible pose, meaning the most exposure of the skin. However, if excessive damage is done to an animal that is otherwise special to the hunter, he might have to choose alternative methods of mounting. If the animal's body area has been damaged extensively, a half mount or shoulder mount may be the only option. If heavy damage is done to one side, then you can choose to mount the animal with the damaged side facing the wall or in a lying-down position. If only one leg is damaged, you might be able to display the animal in a field scene where grass or brush can be placed around the leg to hide the damaged area. As long as you're careful not to put an animal into an odd or unnatural pose, you can use your imagination to hide these imperfections.

Believing that nothing is a lost cause is not unreasonable. By using the knowledge acquired from this book, as well as your own personal experience, you should have no trouble determining some method of preserving a prize animal, as long as there is something left to work with. The hunter mentioned on page 4 who shot his bear in the head, inflicting considerable damage, didn't get to mount his prize. So he simply had the skin made into a rug. Sometimes the circumstances of the hunt don't allow for the most imaginative taxidermy.

3. Make certain the skin being mounted is properly preserved, cleaned, and degreased if necessary.

This subject can't be stressed enough. You will quickly find that many of the initial problems encountered can be reduced or eliminated by following these guidelines completely. Proper field care and preservation should help reduce the chance of slippage. Proper cleaning eliminates hair that is dull or that clumps together. Once the taxidermist reaches the mounting stage, the skin and hair of his specimen should be clean to the touch without any residue of blood or dirt.

Another must for the taxidermist who chooses the dry-preservative method is the use of a degreaser, mainly for greasy animals such as bears or wild hogs. You won't have to put some mammals through the degreasing process, but a quality degreasing agent will go a long way to enhance the luster and shine of nearly all types of mammal hair.

4. Work carefully, but quickly.

As mentioned on page 7, slippage-causing bacteria are a major concern for those in the taxidermy field. In this book I have suggested that all beginners start with dry preservative. This is because dry preservative is quick, easy, and inexpensive. Though I firmly believe that starting with a quality dry preservative is great, learning with a tanned skin is also acceptable, and can actually be helpful in the sense that a properly tanned skin is able to take much more abuse during the mounting process than one which has been dry-preserved. No matter which method of preservation you choose, it is best to remember that any raw skin, whether it is being dry-preserved or slated to be fleshed then salted, should be handled as quickly

as possible to avoid slippage. The longer that a raw skin is handled, the greater the risk that slippage will occur.

To combat this, work with the skin as quickly as possible,
and don't thaw and refreeze a skin more than once before finishing a project. Additionally, if you are concerned that a cape
or life-size skin you are working with is on the brink of slippage, take action. After turning the eyes, nose, lips, and ears,
salt it all quickly, allow it to dry for a couple of days, and then
send it to a commercial tannery, which will have a much better
chance of salvaging the cape or life-size skin. Just remember
that salting and sending a skin to a commercial tannery *can't*
be done if a dry preservative has already been applied.

5. Cut seams as accurately as you can.

You're going to do a lot of sewing to finish a mount. Poor,
sloppy sewing can be the downfall of an otherwise great
mount. To avoid this, ensure that all seams are tight and well
placed. The seam that is used most in commercial taxidermy—
which is any taxidermy not for competition—is a baseball
stitch. To complete a baseball stitch, pierce the skin on one side
of the seam and tie the end of the thread off securely with a
couple overhand knots. Continue by inserting the needle
through the opposite underside of the skin, bring the needle
out the hair side, and then cross over the seam and repeat the
stitch on this side. In through the skin side, out from the hair
side, back and forth, until complete. Keep the stitches as short
and tight as possible. Tie each end off securely and the seam
should present no problems.

Another trick once the seam is complete is to tap it lightly
against the manikin using a small hammer. This will help flatten
it a bit. You can also brush the hair flat in its natural direction,
then tack a small piece of cardboard along the seam, which will
prevent the hair along the seam from standing on end as the
drying takes place. To better understand this, imagine hair on a

dog, or any other animal. The hair tends to flow or lay in a certain direction. If you stroke a horse or a dog in the opposite direction of the hair flow, the hair will bend and turn upwards appearing unruly. On the other hand, if you stroke the animal in the appropriate direction the hair will appear natural and undisturbed. Same goes for the sewing process. After sewing, some hair may be sticking straight up, away from the flow of the natural hair pattern. This is due to the sewing process. To combat this, comb the hair in an appropriate direction, then lay a cardboard piece on top. This will force the hair to remain in a preferred direction until the skin is dry at which time the hair will remain in its intended direction.

6. Bring the mount to life by feigning movement.

After lengthy study of reference materials you will find that putting motion, no matter how small, into a mount can significantly improve its look. Most learning taxidermists, however, are hesitant to put much movement into their mounts, which is understandable—you're much more interested in getting the basics down and getting them right.

But here's a little taxidermist's secret: use the tail. Most animals are constantly broadcasting their feelings with their tails. Whitetails raise their tails in warning. Cougars flick their tails as they study their prey. Foxes wrap their tails around themselves. About the only animal that doesn't show a lot of tail motion is a bear. So with a little study of reference material, you can impart some apparent motion to the tail, and you'll be surprised how much life it will bring to an otherwise static-looking early mount.

The ears are another point of opportunity. I see many mounts that have both ears in a forward-straight position. This is fine for a statue, but most animals are constantly monitoring their surroundings. They swivel their ears, sometimes one at a time, sometimes both to the rear. Animals will also pull their ears tight to their head when scared or angered, so keep this in mind. A mount that portrays movement will be much more convincing to an onlooker. This goes for any portion of the body that can be positioned for movement in the pose desired.

A good example of this is a mount I saw recently of a bobcat leaping for a bird. The mount wasn't extraordinarily impressive in terms of skill level, but the bobcat's tail was swung to one side and the ears were laid back in an aggressive position. For me, this added a great deal of realism to the bobcat's appearance.

7. Dry the feet on the surface to which they will be permanently attached.

This rule generally applies to small game or birds more than it does to big game, but the same goes for any life-size animal. A detail that I find overlooked by some taxidermists is the attachment of the feet to a base. Many taxidermists complete a mount on a flat, lifeless board, but then transfer it to the actual, formal mount surface and expect it to look as if it is naturally walking along. A good example of this would be a life-size bear mount intended to be placed on a base containing rocks. Naturally, the bear's foot should curve around the rock, tightly gripping it, just as you would grip a baseball. However, if the bear mount was finished on a flat surface and then placed on the rocks later, the finished appearance would be similar to that of a person trying to throw a baseball with a flat, open hand.

To avoid this problem, prepare the actual mount base prior to mounting the skin and manikin. Then, attach the animal to the mount base before it dries and manipulate the feet to conform to this final surface. Sometimes the taxidermist can get away with building the base to suit the critter, but for best results, conform the feet to the premade base.

8. Let your self-confidence grow.

When I talk with other taxidermists, whether they have years of experience or are still in the learning process, I sense that their biggest disadvantage isn't lack of knowledge, but lack of confidence. Confidence can easily make or break a person when it comes to attempting—and completing—any given task, especially a complex one. All of us as taxidermists have gone through the same beginning stages, the frustrations, and the doubts. I can assure you that the taxidermist who wins next year's world, national, or even state championship is struggling today to produce his best work possible. I can also assure you that his first attempt isn't remotely similar to the one that clinches the championship.

When the going gets tough and you feel like this isn't for you, go ahead and quit—just not for good. After a short breather to gather your thoughts, step back into the shop, garage, or basement, and continue. Things will get easier, and your work will get better. And when it's all done, you will have the ultimate satisfaction of completing something you have worked very hard to achieve.

Appendix A: Taxidermy Resources

Quality Supplier: Research Mannikins (www.rmi-online.com)

A highly respected taxidermy supply company is Research Mannikins. They have helped taxidermists worldwide begin their hobbies or their careers. They also have a vast assortment of most any type of taxidermy-related item available. Research Mannikins also offers its customers technical advice from an on-staff taxidermist. Advice such as this can be priceless when you are right in the middle of a pronghorn antelope mount and for some reason, nothing seems to be working. To order a Research Mannikins catalog, call 1–800–826–0654.

Join Your State Taxidermy Association

Long ago, taxidermy was basically a secret art. No books were written, no videos made, and you wouldn't have even considered asking the taxidermist down the street for instruction. But times have changed significantly. Being part of a state taxidermy association means that the wisdom of fellow taxidermists is usually just a phone call away. Most are eager to share how-to instructions and advice with a fellow member, and this is especially true if they know you are new to the art.

Taxidermy associations nationwide hold annual seminars and competitions that are geared toward improving the techniques and craftsmanship of its members, and not at all about trying to put one taxidermist's work above another's. I have no problem with others judging my work, and having others' work win over mine—that's all a matter of the judges' taste. Getting involved in competitive showing pushes you to improve your techniques, pick up tricks, and learn over and over what makes a really good mount. Competitions are a tremendous learning tool, as some of the best taxidermists in the world are asked to critique each mount that has been entered. This is invaluable, because they don't just critique your work—they also elaborate on ways to improve it.

Most taxidermy suppliers can provide the contact information for your local state association. You can also check online at www.nationaltaxidermists.com. Another website, www.taxidermy.net, offers interesting, informative discussion forums, links to the web pages of professional taxidermists, and helpful information about competitions and conventions.

SUBSCRIBE TO *TAXIDERMY TODAY* OR *BREAKTHROUGH* MAGAZINES

Subscribing to these publications can be a tremendous asset. Although they are not geared solely toward big-game taxidermy, each month's issues will contain a great deal of information about a variety of big-game species, as well as small game and various birds. Articles written for these publications outline the most advanced procedures you will find anywhere.

To contact *Breakthrough*, call 1–800–783–7266 or go to www.breakthroughmagazine.com. To contact *Taxidermy Today*, call 1–800–851–7955, or check out www.taxidermy today.com.

Select a Tannery

The best tannery I have worked with is East Coast Tannery, located in Pennsylvania. I must say I have never encountered a problem while working with them, and their customer service is the best. For that reason I highly recommend their services to any newcomers. To contact East Coast Tannery, call 877–TAN–FURS or 215–257–9479. They will be glad to assist you with helpful directions for shipment.

Appendix B: Arizona Elk Hunting

To find out more about elk hunting on the San Carlos Apache Reservation in Arizona, call 1–928–475–2343 or visit their website at www.scatrw.com. To contact Gabriel Jackson of Turnbull Guide Service, call 1–602–391–8806 or contact him at gjackson67@yahoo.com.

Index

Seam sewing
mounting process, 125
Self-confidence, 206–207
Septum insertion
nostrils, 104
tool, 103
Sewing, 204–205
dorsal incision, 53
regulator needles, 27
Sheep
annual harvest rates, 147
Short cuts
shoulder-mount skinning,
49–52
Shoulder mount
adhesive, 162
antelope, 139–158
big game, 40
big-game animals, 159
big game experience, 163
Bondo, 123
cuts, 47, 48
deer, 121–138
elk, 139–158, 155
face modeling, 128
manikins, 126
mounting process,
123–128
problems, 48
skinning, 47–48, 49–52
Shrinkage, 165, 170
Skeletal structure
skinning, 44
Skife knife, 76

Skin, 202
composition, 87
damage, 5
degreasing, 91–92
degreasing methods, 91
detachment, 125
fleshing, 65
fleshing beam, 78
mounting precautions,
203
mounting process, 125
mouth cup junction, 177
neutralization, 92–93
shifting, 154
stretchers, 15
tanning, 87
trophy mounting, 6
Skinning
animal, 6
bear paws, 58–59
big-game animals, 43–64
care guide, 2
7 cuts for shoulder-mount,
49–52
eye-to-nose
measurements, 45
fleshing, 43
hoofed animals, 57–58
hunters, 44
knives, 11, 57
life-size, 52–55
life-size mounts, 45
ligaments, 41
methods, 47–55